DARLINGTON
IN 100 DATES

CHRIS LLOYD

To Julie,
With best wishes,

Chris Lloyd

The
History
Press

First published 2015

The History Press
The Mill, Brimscombe Port
Stroud, Gloucestershire, GL5 2QG
www.thehistorypress.co.uk

British Library Cataloguing in Publication Data.
A catalogue record for this book is available from the British Library.

ISBN 978 0 7509 5207 1

Typesetting and origination by The History Press
Printed in Great Britain

Contents

Introduction & Acknowledgements   4

Darlington in 100 Dates   5

Bibliography   127

Introduction & Acknowledgements

These are 100 of my favourite stories that have appeared in my 'Memories' column in *The Northern Echo* since I started writing it twenty-five years ago. Back then, I was just a trainee and it was merely a picture caption which no one wanted to write; now I'm Deputy Editor and it is a twelve-page weekly supplement that is one of the most popular parts of the paper.

I became interested in the local history of Darlington as I tried to understand the town where I had generously been offered a job after leaving university, despite only having set foot a couple of times on Bank Top station platform – which means, I now know, that I got a step closer than Queen Victoria, who only gazed out of her carriage window.

I'm not sure I am any closer to my desired comprehension but I think I have uncovered some great stories – fascinating and often funny – about a great place.

My researches often start in Darlington Centre for Local Studies, and successive editors have always supported me, most notably Peter Barron, who currently keeps W.T. Stead's chair warm. My wife, Petra, has been with me every step of the way, and I have been guided by my readers, whose knowledge, interest, enthusiasm and ability to stay awake during my talks never ceases to amaze me.

My thanks to them all, and I'm already looking forward to finding out about the next 100.

Chris Lloyd, 2015

DARLINGTON
IN 100 DATES

19 July

Margaret, the 13-year-old daughter of Henry VII, slept in the Bishop's Manor House in Darlington on her way to meet her new husband, James IV of Scotland, for the first time. Margaret's hand had been part of the deal that had sealed the 1502 Treaty of Perpetual Peace between the feuding countries. She married James by proxy (i.e. the bridegroom was absent) in Richmond Palace on 25 January 1503, and then journeyed to meet him.

She rode on horseback, but when she came within 3 miles of a town, she jumped into a richly decorated bed and was carried in style by two footmen. The footmen picked their way over the Tees into Neasham, where the Abbess of Neasham, the Bishop of Durham and a 'fayr company', including forty horsemen, offered her a cross to kiss.

She was conveyed into Darlington, greeting knights and sheriffs on the roadside, and at the gates of St Cuthbert's church, the vicar and 'folks of the church' welcomed her.

Margaret slept in the Bishop's Palace – where the town hall is today – and a special lock was fitted to her chamber door (for centuries, its key was one of Darlington's most prized possessions). Next morning, she left for Durham 'in fayr array'.

The Treaty of Perpetual Peace lasted ten years before James invaded England in 1513.

(Longstaffe: *History and Antiquities of Darlington*)

7 May

Between the hours of 12 a.m. and 1 a.m. there took hold 'a most fierce and terrible fire as [if] it had been wildfire, which burned most faire houses in the Towne. It took good holde of pitch, tar, rossen, flax, gunpowder and such like commodities, and ceased not until it had burned 273 houses.'

Fanned by a 'boisterous wind', the timber houses rapidly burned. The wells were dry because of a drought, so people had either to run to the Skerne for water, or toss liquids like milk and beer onto the flames.

Much of High Row and Skinnergate was destroyed, including the house of the leading Eure family. Prosperous merchant Francis Oswell lost goods valued at £1,000, and in total the fire was said to have caused £20,000 of damage.

Although the area around St Cuthbert's church was untouched, the Great Fire of Darlington rendered about 800 of Darlington's 1,200 inhabitants homeless. They sought shelter in barns in nearby villages. A pamphlet, 'Lamentable Newes from the Towne of Darnton', told of the 'poor distressed people' in need of help. Their distress deepened in the autumn when the farmers evicted them from the barns so they could store their harvest.

Although the town was rebuilt on the old medieval street layout, it took several generations for Darlington to recover.

('Memories', *The Northern Echo*, 2011)

26 July

George Swalwell was the last person to be publicly executed in Darlington. He had been sentenced to death in Durham three days earlier for treason as he refused to renounce his Catholicism. He was trussed to a cart and taken to his hometown, where four priests beat him with a rod across the Market Place to the gallows on Bakehouse Hill.

'To terrify him the more, they led him by two great fires, the one made for burning his bowels, the other for boiling his quarters,' recorded Bishop Richard Challoner.

The rope was put around Swalwell's neck and, as he urged Catholics in the crowd to pray for him, he was pushed off the ladder. He was cut down before he lost consciousness and the hangman 'drew him along by the rope yet alive, and there dismembered and bowelled him, and cast his bowels into the fire', said the bishop.

> At the taking out of his heart, he lifted up his left hand to his head, which the hangman laid down again; and when the heart was cast into the fire, the same hand laid itself over the open body ... Then the hangman cut off his head and held it up saying: 'Behold the head of a traitor!' His quarters, after they were boiled in a cauldron, were buried in the baker's dunghill.

('Memories', *The Northern Echo*, 2002)

14 May

King James VI of Scotland was making his journey south to London to be crowned King James I of England when he came across the stunning view of Teesdale, to the west of Darlington. At Bolam, he stopped and sat with his back against an ancient, arthritic stone finger and drank in the view.

'I have taken possession of the promised land,' he sighed. 'It is a bonnie, bonnie country.' As he was sitting cross-legged, the stone finger was immediately nicknamed 'Leg's Cross' (another explanation is that the stone was erected by the Romans' 20th Legion of Piercebridge, but the weathering of time meant that only 'LEG X' survived of their carving).

The king adjourned to Walworth Castle for the night, where his host was Elizabeth Jennison. Her late husband, Thomas, had been Queen Elizabeth I's Auditor General for Ireland and had restored the ruined castle in the 1580s.

The king 'was so bountifully entertained that it gave his excellency very high contentment', says a contemporary account. 'After his quiet repose there that night and part of the next day, he took leave of her with many princely gratulations.'

In the seventeenth century, the Saxon village of Walworth, which was to the north of the castle, was cleared by the castle owners to improve their view. Since 1981, the castle has been a hotel.

('Memories', *The Northern Echo*, 2005)

5 June

Xpofer Simpson, a labourer from Thornaby, was discovered strangled near the confluence of the Baydale Beck and the River Tees at Low Coniscliffe. The alarm was raised and Xpofer's nephew, weaver Ralph Simpson, was seized at Aldborough St John and dragged back to the scene where deputy coroner Francis Raisbie swore in fourteen men as the jury.

They heard that Xpofer and Ralph had been to Gunnerside to buy a little black horse for 10*s*. Witnesses reported seeing them en route, but 'before the sunne did arise', Ralph was spotted alone. Constable Thomas Emerson turned out Ralph's pockets and found 'a cord made of throumes (the warp ends of weaver's web) which was bloody'.

The jury reported: 'Wee applied the cord to the circle that was about the necke of the party murthered, and it did answer unto the circle; and wee caused the said Ralph to handle the bodye; and upon his handlinge and movinge, the body did bleed both at mouth, nose and eares.' As Shakespeare said, 'blood will have blood' – an old belief that a body would bleed afresh when approached by the murderer.

Due to such incontrovertible proof, Ralph was found guilty. He was hanged at Durham before the week was out, and the balladeers made a fortune selling copies of their new composition, 'The Baydayle Banckes Tragedy'.

('Memories', *The Northern Echo*, 2011)

1 December

The Battle of Piercebridge was fought between Royalists led by William Cavendish, 1st Duke of Newcastle upon Tyne, and Colonel John Hotham, a Parliamentarian commander.

Cavendish was marching to Yorkshire with 8,000 men when he discovered 'Hotham's Roundheads' dug in on the high ground of Cliffe on the Yorkshire bank of the Tees. They were a much smaller force: three troops of horsemen and four companies of foot soldiers with two guns, commanded by Captain Hatcher. When the Royalists rushed at Piercebridge, Hatcher rained fire upon them, forcing them to retreat. Roundheads on horseback swept down the steep Yorkshire bank and chased after them, killing several.

Cavendish regrouped. He brought his heavy guns onto the higher Durham bank of the Tees, at Carlbury, and began a bombardment. It destroyed some of Piercebridge's Roman remains, but the Roundheads fled, and Cavendish crossed the bridge unhindered into Yorkshire.

However, his victory came at some cost. Colonel Thomas Howard, grandson of a Cumberland nobleman, was the most senior Royalist officer killed that day. He was buried at St Edwin's church, in High Coniscliffe, although the twenty or so lower ranks that were killed in the rush onto the bridge were lobbed into a common grave near Carlbury Mill, along with their dead horses. Their skeletons were discovered in 1828.

('Memories', *The Northern Echo*, 2011)

22 August

The newly enthroned Bishop of Durham, John Cosin, wrote of the scene that had greeted him in the middle of the River Tees at High Wath, Neasham, when he entered his bishopric for the first time from the south.

More than 1,000 people, many on horseback, stood in the river waiting to present him with the Conyers falchion – the enormous sword that Sir John Conyers once used to slay the Sockburn Worm, or dragon.

The bishop wrote:

> The confluence and alacritie of the gentry, clergy, and other people, was very great, and at my first entrance through the river of Tease, there was scarce any water to be seene for the multitude of horse and men that filled it, when the sword that killed the dragone was delivered to me with all the formality of trumpets, and gunshots, and acclamations that might be made.

Sir John had required the strength of the Holy Spirit to wield the falchion against the 'fiery flying serpent' that had terrorised people in Saxon times, and so the sword represents the strength of the faith of the people of Durham. For centuries, it has been presented to the new bishop when he crosses into Durham, although since High Wath closed in 1790, the ceremony has been performed on Croft Bridge – most recently in 2014.

(Longstaffe, and Lloyd: *Rockliffe*)

24 September

On this day, Sir Gilbert Gerard, the High Sherriff of Durham, died. His wife Dame Mary is the most likely source of the story of Darlington's most famous ghost.

Mary and her younger sister Frances were the daughters of John Cosin, the Bishop of Durham. They married brothers, Sir Gilbert and Sir Charles Gerard (or Jarratt), and during the English Civil War (1642–51), they moved into the Bishop's Palace in the Leadyard (now the location of the town hall) for safety. But Puritan soldiers burst in, demanding money. Lady Gerard protested that she had none – so they tried to take the jewel-encrusted ring on her finger. But no matter how hard they pulled, it would not come. Hearing Lady Gerard's husband approaching, a soldier hacked off her arm with his knife, and hastily departed. Blood spurting from her wound, Lady Gerard slumped down the wall and died.

Days later, her arm, minus the ring, was found by a fisherman in the Skerne, and until the palace was demolished in the 1930s, a red stain down a wall could never be covered by whitewash. Lady Gerard is regularly seen in a long white silk dress in the Leadyard, searching for her lost limb:

> The lady who in violence died
> Left her blood that none could hide,
> Her desolate vigil still to keep,
> While Darlington folk are sound asleep.

('Memories', *The Northern Echo*, 2001)

16 April

Lying paralysed on the battlefield at Culloden, where the English had just routed the Scots, soldier Sam Addy confessed to Jack Langstraffe that he had murdered Cicely Kirby on Blackwell Lane, Darlington, a few days earlier when the English army had broken its journey north in the town.

Langstraffe, who had lost part of his arm, lunged at Addy, for he had been dating Cicely in secret. Theirs had been a love that could not reveal itself because she was a lowly maid lodging in a house beside the Skerne, whereas he was the son of wealthy Blackwell farmer.

A stretcher party separated the two men and carried them to a field hospital where Addy, his back broken, explained how harmless horseplay had ended when Cicely fell and bashed her head on a tree root. In haste, he'd finished her off by strangling her with her scarf, and burying her in a shallow roadside grave. As Addy struggled for breath, the hospital tent filled with a bright white light with a ghostly green girl at its centre. Then he died. Similar spooky sightings have been reported in Blackwell Grange on the anniversary of the Battle of Culloden.

On 2 September 1935, workmen in Blackwell Lane found a young woman's skeleton in a shallow roadside grave. It was almost 200 years old.

('Memories', *The Northern Echo*, 2000)

21 May

Mathematician William Emerson died in Hurworth, seven days after his 71st birthday. A great eccentric – he wore his shirts back to front to stop the wind blowing in through the buttonholes, and he invented 'shin-covers' which enabled him to sit close to the fire without burning the lower part of his legs – he wrote mathematical textbooks that inspired in Thomas Jefferson, the third President of the United States, a lifelong love of maths.

He tested his theorems before publishing his books. He researched *A Treatise of Navigation*, which was about the angles sailing ships needed to be to the wind, by standing waist-deep in the Tees with lots of boys, examining the movements of their toy boats.

For *The Art of Dialling* – about the creation of accurate sundials – he and his assistant John Hunter installed at least thirty sundials on Hurworth's south-facing houses. A couple remain.

One day, when Hunter was mending Emerson's roof on The Green, a carriageload of Cambridge University professors arrived with an apparently unsolvable mathematical problem. Emerson took one look, called Hunter off the roof and asked him to provide the solution. Hunter chalked the answer on his hat, Emerson declared it correct and handed the hat to the professors, telling them to send it back when they'd worked out how to reach the same conclusion.

(Longstaffe, and Lloyd: *Rockliffe*)

20 November

A nationwide hunt came to an end when Gabriel Thornton, an old countryman, pulled on the bridle of a horse tearing through Neasham. The rider, Andrew Robinson Stoney Bowes, pointed his pistol at Gabriel's head and was about to pull the trigger when Christopher Smith, the village constable, knocked Bowes off his horse and freed the lady who, wearing only a nightdress, was tied to the saddle. She was Bowes' estranged wife, Lady Mary Eleanor Strathmore.

Eleven days earlier Bowes, the MP for Newcastle, had kidnapped Lady Mary in London's Oxford Street and had carried her on horseback to Streatlam Castle – between Darlington and Barnard Castle – where he had tried to force her to drop her divorce case.

With rescuers closing in, Bowes had tied her to his horse and set off on a mad chase around the Pennines. They covered at least 180 miles in eight days, and once, possibly twice, Bowes had stopped in a solicitor's house next to the Sun Inn, in the centre of Darlington. From there, he had charged towards Sockburn, but Gabriel spotted him, with the muddy and bloodied lady tied on the back wearing a man's greatcoat.

Arrested, Bowes was divorced by Lady Mary and he spent the rest of his days in a debtors' prison. When Constable Smith died in 1797, his widow received an anonymous envelope containing £5 – apparently from the Strathmore family.

('Memories', *The Northern Echo*, 2000)

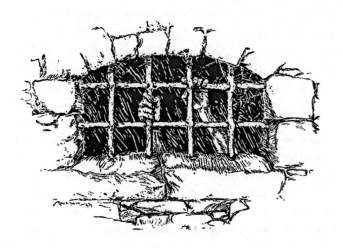

19 February

Having travelled more than 3,000 miles in six years, the Durham Ox made its last personal appearance in Oxford.

It was born in March 1796 at the Ketton farm, north of Darlington, belonging to the Colling brothers, Robert and Charles. They were leading breeders of supersize shorthorn cattle – their largest monster, Comet, the first £1,000 ox, was born in 1804.

On 4 May 1801, when the Durham Ox weighed 214 stone (1,360kg), it was sold for £250 to John Day of Rotherham, a farmer showman. He built it a luxurious padded carriage, which was pulled by six horses, and turned it into a touring freakshow. It spent much of 1802 starring in London, where takings were £97 a day, and in late 1803 it returned to Darlington for one night only before a twelve-night extravaganza in Newcastle.

'My wife, who rode with him in the carriage, found him harmless as a fawn and familiar as a lapdog,' wrote Mr Day in his memoirs. 'He was surprisingly agile for one so large.' Merchandise, such as prints, china plates and models, were produced as Mr Day milked his ox for publicity, and pubs – even in the Australian goldfields – were named after it.

But on that fateful day in 1807, the Ox slipped while exiting its carriage and dislocated a hip. After eight weeks, the 271-stone behemoth was still in pain so three butchers slaughtered it.

('Memories', *The Northern Echo*, 2008)

22 March

Revd Thomas Le Mesurier, vicar of Haughton-le-Skerne, became the centre of national attention when he punched a 14-year-old boy so hard in the mouth that he lost a tooth.

In 1804, Le Mesurier had been the private chaplain and advisor to Lord Sidmouth, the former Tory prime minister notorious for praising the troops that, in 1819, had killed fifteen working-class protestors during the Peterloo Massacre in Manchester.

Because of Le Mesurier's right-wing affiliations and because Durham's Whig MP, John 'Radical Jack' Lambton supported many of the protestors' demands, the massacre became an issue during the 1820 election in Darlington. One Wednesday in Lent, a pro-Lambton parade passed through Haughton and the chants of 'Lambton forever!' were so loud that they could be heard in the church. Le Mesurier, in his flowing black robes, dashed out and confronted Robert Richardson, the son of a shoemaker.

'Forgetting his own character, and the temper of his profession, he struck a blow which brought blood to the mouth of the plaintiff and loosed one of his teeth,' said *The Times*. 'A clergyman ought to have found a different mode of stopping the mouth of a boy of 14.'

In court, the only debate was whether Richardson had 'jockled' his tooth out to exaggerate his injuries. The punching parson was found guilty, and fined £10.

('Memories', *The Northern Echo*, 2010)

19 April

At about 5 p.m., two strangers approached Edward Pease's home in Northgate. They'd set off early that morning on horseback from Northumberland. At Newcastle, they'd caught a stagecoach for Stockton 'by nip' – paying the driver a backhander rather than the full fare. From Stockton, they'd walked 12 miles across farm and field, following the path of the proposed 'railway or tramroad'.

One story says they had 'walked barefoot to Darlington, shoeing themselves near the Bulmer Stone' before crossing the road to Mr Pease's home. Barefoot would have saved their shoe leather, although another version has them stopping at the stone to take their shoes off in deference to the great Quaker entrepreneur they were approaching. Barefoot or not, it did not matter: Edward's servant sent them away as they had no appointment.

Edward, meanwhile, was waiting upstairs for news from London about whether the Parliamentary Bill granting him permission to build his 'railway or tramroad' had received Royal Assent. He heard the commotion, came downstairs and invited the men into his kitchen – which is today a kebab takeaway and a pizza parlour. There, on a pink-and-cream sofa, the callers – George Stephenson and Nicholas Wood – convinced Pease that the project should be a railway rather than a tramroad, and that it should be steam-powered and not horse-powered. Thus the Stockton and Darlington Railway was born, and history was made.

('Memories', *The Northern Echo*, 2000)

27 September

The locomotive, or steam horse as it was more generally termed, gave 'note of preparation' by 'some heavy respirations which seemed to excite astonishment and alarm among the Johnny Raws', reported the *Durham County Advertiser* on the opening of the Stockton and Darlington Railway. 'When a portion of steam was led off, they fled in affright, accompanied by women and young children under the idea that some horrible explosion was about to take place.'

It didn't. Instead Locomotion No. 1, driven by George Stephenson's brother James, pulled an 80-ton train of thirty-eight wagons carrying passengers as well as coal and flour from Shildon to Darlington at a top speed of 15mph. The 553 passengers, said *The Northern Echo* in 1875, had 'never before seen the trees, fences and hedges glide away so rapidly, or did their ribbons and handkerchiefs ever flicker in such a wind as they did that day.'

As brakes hadn't been perfected, railwaymen stood on the couplings ready to jam pieces of wood into the wheels should the need arise, and when there was a derailment, everyone jumped off and pushed the wagon back onto the tracks.

In the luxury of the 'Experiment' – a shed on some pram wheels which was the world's first passenger carriage – travelled all the railway directors except Edward Pease, whose favourite son, Isaac, had died the night before, aged 22.

('Memories', *The Northern Echo*, 2000)

1 February

It was on this day that Jonathan Martin, who worked for six years in Darlington, torched York Minster. He came from near Hexham, and was press-ganged into the Royal Navy in 1804, aged 22. After six years, he escaped and settled at Norton, near Stockton, where he began having visions and gained a reputation for storming Anglican pulpits mid-sermon. His estranged wife informed the authorities in 1818 that he intended to shoot the Bishop of Durham, and he was sent to a Gateshead asylum. He escaped and settled in Darlington where he courted a saddler's housekeeper in Tubwell Row.

In 1825, he wrote an autobiographical pamphlet entitled 'The Life of Jonathan Martin, of Darlington, Tanner', and for three years he toured the region, selling 14,000 copies of the 1*s* pamphlet, until visions of fires took over his mind.

After evensong in York Minster, he hid while everyone left and then made a fire of hymnbooks and gold tassels on the bishop's pew. Knocking out a window, he escaped down a bell rope. By noon next day, the minster was so well ablaze that its four-teenth-century roof came crashing down. Martin was arrested near Hexham five days later. He spent the remaining seven years of his life in a lunatic asylum in Lambeth, proclaiming: 'It was not me … but my God did it.'

('Memories', *The Northern Echo*, 2005)

30 October

The Earl of Tankerville stopped for Sunday lunch at the King's Head Hotel en route for Chillingham Castle, Northumberland. He was accompanied by his daughter, Lady Corisande, and her husband, Lord Malmesbury. Their lordships had just helped defeat the Great Reform Bill, which would have extended the vote to more ordinary people.

Returning to their carriage after lunch, 'a storm of stones assailed us and a furious mob tried to stop us', said Malmesbury in his memoirs. 'When I saw what was coming, I pulled my wife under the seat, which saved her from a large paving stone which struck the place where she had been sitting.' With Lady Corisande cowering, the coach 'ran the gauntlet at full gallop until we cleared the town', but was badly damaged.

'The outrage was committed deliberately and with preparation for the first Peer who passed Darlington after having voted against the reform Bill,' wrote Malmesbury, who was Foreign Secretary in the 1850s. 'The stones stood in heaps ready, piled like ammunition, and the victims were to be thrown into the river.'

But hairdresser Jonathan Dresser recalled that the aristocrats had made incendiary gestures at the crowd. He said: 'Such unwarranted putting of thumbs, twiddling of fingers and slapping of thighs was enough to inflame even the most mild-mannered of men to riot.'

(Malmesbury: *Memoirs of an Ex-Minister*)

4 February

North Road station ticket clerk Thomas Munro Winter shot himself through the head in the station toilets. 'He was observed for some time past to be in a desponding state,' reported the *Durham County Advertiser*. Mr Winter, 29, and married for four months, had recently been accused – unjustly in his eyes – of selling a ticket to a drunken passenger. His body was laid out in the porter's cellar beneath the platform.

One midnight some years later, nightwatchman James Durham had an experience in the same porter's cellar which journalist W.T. Stead called 'the most remarkable of all the stories of ghosts which touch'.

Wearing the same uniform as Mr Winter – 'a cut away coat with gilt buttons, a stand up collar and a scotch cap' – a ghost punched James in the face and then its black dog – just like Mr Winter's – bit his leg. James punched back, but his fist went straight through the apparition and hit the wall. The ghost was knocked backwards, and hurriedly disappeared with its dog into the coalhouse. The only evidence James had was his skinned knuckles – the dog had left no bitemarks.

Edward 'father of the railways' Pease, who had known Durham and so knew the accuracy of James' descriptions, accepted the veracity of James' story.

('Memories', *The Northern Echo*, 2000)

28 September

Queen Victoria, the first monarch of the railway age, 'most graciously consented' to break her journey from Balmoral to the Isle of Wight and stopped briefly in Darlington.

'The Bank Top Station was repainted, and hung with evergreens and banners, platforms and terraces were prepared, floral crowns furnished, and all the petty splendour a rural town could muster was brought to bear on the event,' wrote historian William Longstaffe. Thousands turned out. All the church bells pealed and, at 1.35 p.m., as the royal train appeared, the band struck up the Royal Anthem.

But Victoria did not alight. She sent her Home Secretary, Sir George Grey, to accept the bouquets and gifts. She was seen through the window wearing 'a light plaid shawl and white silk bonnet, trimmed in the simplest manner', sniffing at the bouquet prepared in the Grange Road garden of John Harrison. 'After remaining about 15 minutes in the station, the train moved slowly through the crowded lines of spectators for York, amid repeated peals of cheers,' said Longstaffe. 'The day was completely a holiday, the shops were closed, and a glorious bonfire and heaps of noisy fireworks, with an illumination or two, made night cheerful.'

The queen, though, was not amused. Even though the Bank Top shed had been repainted, she expressed surprise that the birthplace of the railways did not possess something more grand.

('Memories', *The Northern Echo*, 2011)

23 May

The *Felix*, with a crew of nineteen, set sail from Stranraer to discover the fate of explorer Sir John Franklin. He had been gone for five years on an Arctic mission to find the Northwest Passage, a putative short cut that joins the Atlantic with the Pacific.

The *Felix* was captained by veteran explorer John Ross, 73, many of whose expeditions had been sponsored by the gin distiller Sir Felix Booth, after whom he had named large parts of the Arctic. Indeed, Sir Felix had chipped in another £1,000 for the rescue mission.

Although Ross, often fortified with his sponsor's product to keep out the cold, was not successful, he returned with the news that three skeletons belonging to Sir John's men had been discovered to the north of Boothia, hinting at terrible calamity.

The crew of the *Felix* then broke up. The ship's doctor, David Porteous, landed a job in the new village of Middleton St George that was growing beside an ironworks to the east of Darlington. Ironworking being dangerous, the doctor prospered, and in 1876 built himself a sturdy villa-cum-surgery, with two iron balconies and a pair of conservatories. He named it after the small ship on which he had sailed to the Arctic, and so today the people of Middleton St George are treated in Felix House.

('Memories', *The Northern Echo*, 2003)

21 December

'Invited to the Procters' this evening to see what is called a Christmas tree,' wrote Edward Pease, 86, in his diary. 'I did not feel inclined to go. About 70 were present.' In turning down the invitation from Misses Jane, Barbara and Elizabeth Procter, grumpy Edward missed out on a seasonal piece of local history: the first recorded Christmas tree in Darlington.

The trees only became fashionable in 1848 when the *Illustrated London News* pictured Queen Victoria, Prince Albert and their children beside a candle-covered fir.

The first Darlington tree was in the Procters' boarding school for girls at No. 11, Houndgate. The following year, the sisters moved their school to Polam Hall, where it remains. The Polam Hall Christmas Tree Party became the highlight of Darlington's festive calendar, with the pupils covering it in numbered gifts. Their guests drew numbers in a raffle and found their presents on the tree. Great fun ensued as everyone swapped gifts until they had something suitable.

Edward was never reconciled to such hilarity. His diary of 28 December 1855, found him at his son Joseph's home. He wrote: 'The evening spent less to my comfort than usually, the levity etc of what is termed a Christmas tree was below that which belongs to those who have attained to maturer years.'

(*The Diaries of Edward Pease*)

31 July

Edward Pease, 'the father of the railways', died aged 90 in his home in Northgate, which is now a pizza parlour and a kebab takeaway.

Edward was born in Bull Wynd. He began his career in textiles, riding hundreds of miles to buy fleeces for his Priestgate mills and, ironically for a pacifist Quaker, he made his fortune during the Napoleonic Wars, as his mills were busy for fifteen years providing yarn for uniforms.

A fire at his mill in 1817 threw his 600 employees – nearly 10 per cent of town's population – out of work, and encouraged him to diversify. He took an interest in plans to connect the south Durham coalfield with the sea, and began investing in 1818. To protect his investment, he took control, and risks – he decided it was to be a steam-powered, locomotive-driven railway, while others were still imagining it being horse-drawn.

The Northern Echo wrote in 1875: 'He was supreme; what he could not do by influence he effected by sheer weight of votes; and hence for many a long year he was regarded as the King of the Railway, whose sovereignty extended over every department.'

A strict Quaker, he grappled uneasily with the luxurious lifestyles that his offspring enjoyed due to the immense wealth brought to them by the railways which, when he died, girdled the globe.

('Memories', *The Northern Echo*, 2010)

9 March

Punch magazine published a cartoon attacking the Bishop of Durham over the Cheese Affair: 'a nasty stink at Haughton-le-Skerne', it claimed.

By an accident of history, the village vicar was extremely wealthy; he was paid £1,300 a year, nearly four times as much as clerics in Darlington. In 1861, it was expected that the new Bishop of Durham, the Right Revd Henry Montagu Villiers, would reform the salary structure but, instead, he announced that the new vicar, who would take the whole salary, was Revd Edward Cheese, 28. Mr Cheese had been in Holy Orders for only three years and happened to have married the bishop's only daughter, Amy Maria, a few months earlier. This, said the *Darlington Telegraph*, was much 'to the chagrin of petitioners and the excitement in the public mind'.

The *Manchester Guardian* accused the bishop of 'gross nepotism' and *Punch* launched its cartoon parodies. It asserted that Revd Cheese came from an old Cheshire family. It punned:

> Our Bishop's really too anxious to please,
> When we ask for bread, he gives us Cheese.

The stress of the national outcry drove the bishop to a premature death six months later, aged 48, although Mr Cheese served his parish for twenty-three years, becoming widely admired, until he died at 51 – not a ripe old age.

('Memories', *The Northern Echo*, 2009)

21 March

A performance at the new Theatre Royal in Northgate raised money to mount the Crimean War cannon in South Park, which was in the middle of a bitter local battle that lasted longer than the Crimean War itself.

Nationally, pacifist Quakers had objected to the war, and in January 1854 they sent three emissaries, led by Henry Pease of Pierremont, on a winter dash to St Petersburg to plead with the Russian tsar for peace. The war broke out while Henry was away, and *The Times* newspaper branded him a traitor for consorting with the enemy.

In 1857, after the war, the Peases' opponents asked the government for a captured cannon to commemorate it, but when the cannon arrived, the Peases dumped it in long grass in the park. The pro-cannon lobby fought long and hard to get the cannon erected properly, and eventually forced the Peases to back down, but even today, the cannon has minimal signage because the Peases did not want to glorify a war they opposed.

It is actually a carronade – a naval cannon. One trunnion bears its serial number – 19,632 – and says that it is a 24lb gun made in 1824. The other trunnion reads: 'ALKSND ZVD NACH. FULLON', showing it was manufactured under the direction of a Mr Fullon at the Alexandrovsky factory in Petrozavodsk.

('Memories', *The Northern Echo*, 2005- 2011)

10 June

The Fothergill Fountain was unveiled in the centre of Bondgate. It was a memorial to Dr John Fothergill, who regularly prescribed a long drink of cold, fresh water for his patients, and who for twenty-three years had been president of the Darlington Total Abstinence Society. After his death, the society held a competition to design a memorial which was won by Septimus Hird, 17, the son of a pub landlord – he lived in the Green Tree Inn, Skinnergate – and who, tragically, had drowned while swimming in the sea at Redcar days after entering the competition. So before they could build the Fothergill Memorial Fountain, they had to erect the Hird Memorial Obelisk in West Cemetery.

The fountain's unveiling ceremony, in front of 'a vast concourse of people' was embarrassingly interrupted by John Watson. A painter, Mr Watson was said to be 'three sheets in the wind' – despite it only being 1 p.m. He loudly gave a 'sort of running commentary' on the proceedings, according to the *Darlington and Stockton Times*, and then with 'a heavy hiccup vented his dissatisfaction' with the concept of temperance.

Nevertheless, the fountain was up and running – running so much that it overflowed, churning the earthen street into an ankle-deep muddy morass. In 1875, it was moved to the entrance of South Park, where it remains.

(Lloyd: *A Walk in the Park*)

13 March

Thomas Mitchell, 58, died three days after being run over on the controversial Darlington Street Railroad. The unfortunate ironworker, who was 'rather dull of hearing and had bad sight', had had his right leg 'sadly mutilated' by a horse-drawn tramcar while he was crossing Northgate outside the Railway Tavern.

The American-style tramcar, which ran at 11mph from North Road station to the Market Place, was the third in the country. It opened on 1 January 1862, promoted by the Pease family in conjunction with the American eccentric George Francis Train, who famously travelled around the world in eighty days.

Its rails made it deeply unpopular with horse-owners, who spilled coals and parked wagons full of steaming manure across it. During 'the Northgate blockade', they padlocked their carts so the tramcars couldn't get by, causing driver James Temple Mangles to flog his horses in a bid to get them round the obstruction. Magistrates agreed he wasn't cruel, but instead fined him 21s for driving them onto the pavement.

Then a tramcar ran over a prize greyhound. Its owner, auctioneer Charles Miller, sued the Peases for £50. At the Durham Summer Assizes in July 1864, they argued that the Streetcar Company was liable and not themselves, but the company couldn't pay, so its two trams – named *Nelson* and *Wellington* – ceased running on 1 January 1865.

('Memories', *The Northern Echo*, 2008)

2 May

At 7 a.m. John Wrightson, landlord of the Sun Inn, bought a leg of mutton from Jack Crawford – the first purchase in Darlington's controversial Covered Market.

Mr Wrightson had probably dashed over when he heard the market was beginning to trade because he wanted to cause embarrassment for the Local Board of Health. Its members had commissioned fellow Quaker, Alfred Waterhouse of Manchester, to build an indoor market with town hall and clock tower against the wishes of the townspeople.

The controversy deepened when, on 9 December 1863, during an agricultural show in the half-built market, the floor had given way, catapulting three large prize cattle and ten men into the cellar 12ft below. Farmer Robert Robson of Newton Morrell died two days later of his injuries and the coroner blamed the architect.

However, the ruling Quakers managed to pin the blame on a flawed piece of iron wrought by a local ironfounder. Thus exonerated, 30-year-old Waterhouse became one of the greatest architects of his generation, but it left the Peases and Backhouses so red-faced that they wanted no more fuss surrounding the market, which was why Mr Wrightson dashed over, to make the first purchase (and a big fuss). 'There was no opening ceremony,' noted the *Darlington and Stockton Times*. 'The only official act was the apprehension of a couple of pickpockets who, by way of inauguration, tried their hands at a lady's pocket and got them into a pair of handcuffs.'

('Memories', *The Northern Echo*, 2013)

26 September

The finishing touches to Darlington's iconic clock tower were applied at 11 p.m. when the clock face was backlit by naphtha gas for the first time. Unfortunately, the two men carrying out the trial upset their bucket of naphtha and set fire to the wooden floor upon which they were standing and the ladder up which they had climbed. The crowd gathered below in Tubwell Row saw flames come shooting out of the portholes – rather than the illuminated dial they had expected – and sent up buckets of water from the fountain. 'We understand that the man who took the principal part in extinguishing the flames was burnt about the hands,' reported the *Darlington and Stockton Times*.

Once the men got the gas going properly, they discovered that naphtha burns with a green hue. The original dial was red, and the hands were golden. It looked like something from a horror show, so the townspeople nicknamed it 'Dracula's Castle'.

The *Darlington Telegraph* fumed: 'The figures are totally indistinguishable. It is much to be regretted that after such a large expenditure of money, what was expected to be a great public convenience is a total failure. Plain white glass and black figures along are required.'

Joseph Pease, who had paid £1,000 to have the clock tower built, dipped deeper into his pocket and paid for a new, legible, clock face.

('Memories', *The Northern Echo*, 2013)

25 October

Charles Dickens learned that his favourite younger brother, Frederick, had died five days earlier in Darlington and that he had missed the funeral. The two had become estranged, but Charles had been Fred's father figure when their real father had been sent to a debtors' prison when they were young.

Fred, eight years younger than Charles, had lived and holidayed with the novelist and his wife, and Charles had regularly bailed Fred out when his debts mounted – Charles even paid off Fred's wife when their marriage ended acrimoniously.

Money eventually caused the estrangement between the brothers, but by then, Fred had latched onto Jonathon Ross Feetum, landlord of the White Horse Tavern in Regent Street, London. In 1862, Feetum inherited a cabinet-making business in Tubwell Row, Darlington, and moved north. Fred came too, and spent the last eight years of his life writing, entertaining and drinking until he died in Elton Parade of asphyxia when an abscess on his right lung burst.

Charles belatedly discovered his brother's death and sent a letter to Feetum thanking him for his kindness. It is believed that Charles paid for his brother's headstone in West Cemetery. 'It was a wasted life,' he wrote, 'but God forbid that one should be hard upon it, or upon anything in this world that is not deliberately and coldly wrong.'

('Memories', *The Northern Echo*, 2007)

1 January

The Northern Echo, the country's first halfpenny morning newspaper, was first published in Darlington, born out of a local difficulty for the 'Pease party'. In the 1860s, Henry King Spark wanted a share of the Pease family's political power. He campaigned, successfully, for Darlington to get a democratic town council, and then for it to have its own MP. But he failed to become the council's first mayor so, in November 1868, he stood as an Independent Liberal to be the town's first MP – against the Peases' preferred candidate, the official Liberal Edmund Backhouse.

He used his two local newspapers – the *Darlington and Stockton Times* on a Saturday and the midweek *Darlington Mercury* – to shout out his message in the most libellous way, drowning out the Peases' weekly *Darlington Telegraph*.

A show of hands appeared to elect Mr Spark until Mr Backhouse demanded – legally – a written ballot. In the intervening days, according to Mr Spark, 'from street to street, from ward to ward, the screw was imposed with the most unblushing audacity' by the Pease party. The result was an overwhelming triumph for Mr Backhouse – but within months the Peases had hired the North East's most experienced newspaperman, John Hyslop Bell, to start a regional, daily newspaper to ensure no local weekly paper ever came close to embarrassing them again.

(Lloyd: *Attacking the Devil*)

9 September

Darlington's greatest poet, Ralph Hodgson, was born in Garden Street on this day. A great nature lover, he became a close friend of writers Siegfried Sassoon and Walter de la Mare, and T.S. Eliot tried to persuade him to illustrate *Old Possum's Book of Practical Cats*, upon which the musical *Cats* is based. Hodgson refused – he was more of a dog man – but Eliot still dedicated the book to him. Eliot even wrote a little ditty about him:

How delightful to meet Mr Hodgson!
(Everyone wants to know him)
He has 999 canaries
And round his head finches and fairies
In jubilant rapture skim.
How delightful to meet Mr Hodgson!
(Everyone wants to know him)

Hodgson's father was a prosperous coal merchant until alcoholism took hold, and he spent his last days in the wash house of the family home, in Station Terrace, trying to produce 'Hodgson's Cure-All Aromatic Balm for the Use of Women'. Sadly he died in the late 1870s and Mary, Hodgson's mother, moved the young family to London. Hodgson started as an illustrator and cartoonist. He settled with his second wife in Japan, lecturing in English Literature at a university, and then retired with his third wife to her remote farm in Ohio, where he died in 1961.

('Memories', *The Northern Echo*, 2008)

26 January

Farrier Major Michael 'Spud' Murphy – the only Victoria Cross winner buried in Darlington – was caught stealing 6 bushels of oats and 12lbs of hay in Aldershot. He was stripped of his rank and pension, sentenced to nine months' hard labour, and his family was made homeless.

Murphy, from Tipperary, won his VC on 15 April 1858, during the Indian Mutiny when, despite sustaining five serious injuries, he killed at least five attackers while protecting the body of an officer. He rose through the ranks of the Military Train – the army's transport division – until he was caught supplementing his meagre pay by allowing a sack of oats and a barrowful of hay to leave the barracks. 'For God's sake, look it over this time,' he shouted at his court martial. 'It will ruin me.'

The authorities refused. They ruined him. They even ordered he forfeit his VC. But when Sir Henry Havelock-Allan of Blackwell Grange, himself a veteran of the Indian Mutiny, heard of the case, he took pity on Murphy and offered him employment as a labourer in Darlington. When the VC winner died in Vulcan Street on 4 April 1893, Sir Henry followed his coffin to North Cemetery and paid for his headstone.

In 1920, George V restored Murphy's VC, saying that it was awarded for outstanding split-second valour, not a lifetime of good behaviour.

('Memories', *The Northern Echo*, 2004)

8 February

Joseph Pease, Darlington's greatest son, died aged 72 in his opulent mansion, Southend. He was, according to the *Newcastle Daily Chronicle*, 'head and shoulders above his fellows, in the mine, the manufactory and the mart … a self made magnate … the embodiment of world prosperity … the first of the new aristocracy of England'. Revd Henry Kendall, of Northgate Congregational church, said he 'was the greatest of all men in the North-East of England'.

Just a month earlier, King Charles III of Spain had awarded him the Order of the Grand Cross for distributing thousands of copies of a book about morality among the Spanish workers.

Yet for all his renown and £168 million wealth, Joseph – South Durham's first MP and the founder of Middlesbrough – didn't have health. In 1859, a German oculist had performed an iridectomy on his eye 'without chloroform', or anaesthetic. 'An iridectomy', explained *The Northern Echo*, 'is the making of an incision in the iris, drawing out a few of the capillary vessels and clipping them off – thus relieving the distension and allowing of the optic nerve resuming its usual shape. He suffered much.'

Widowed in 1861, Joseph was blind for his last seven years. Southend is now Bannatyne's Hotel, and the south-facing summer-house, where Joseph in his dotage liked to sit and feel the sun, is where the people of Southend Avenue keep their wheelie bins.

('Memories', *The Northern Echo*, 2007)

17 July

Thirteen years after he had crossed the Niagara Falls on a high wire, the Great Blondin – or Jean-Francois Gravelet, as his parents knew him – was the star attraction at the Grand Fete Champetre held at Polam Hall.'This world-renowned acrobat, whose marvellous exploits on the tight rope evince a daring and intrepidity almost superhuman' put on four shows – two on the Saturday, and two more on the Monday – on a rope tied between two poles on the banks of the Skerne. 'The fine weather on Saturday, and the fame of the performer, drew a very large company, including representatives of most of the influential families of the town and district,' reported *The Northern Echo*.

> The feats that the acrobat performed comprised the astounding acts of walking in a sack, cooking an omelette, carrying a man, riding upon a bicycle, with others of an equally surprising character, all of which were gone through in a manner which fully sustained the reputation of the hero of the Niagara and gave unbounded satisfaction to the spectators.

There is a rumour that Blondin also tied a rope between a chimney on the Comet public house in Hurworth Place on the Durham side of the Tees and a pole in Croft Mill on the North Yorkshire side and edged his way across.

('Memories', *The Northern Echo*, 2004)

4 November

The Northern Echo's editor W.T. Stead visited William Barningham's foundry on Albert Hill, which employed 2,000 men and boys and which had just rolled Japan's first rails.

'In the ruddy light of the furnace fires, a puddler, with rabble or paddle, is working the half molten metal – his features all aglow with the radiating effulgence of the furnace; his naked back and breast wet with sweat-drops,' he wrote. 'A shingler, in his panoply of armour … is holding an incandescent mass of metal for the thrilling blow coming from the steam-impelled hammer.'

Barningham, born in Arkengarthdale, set up his foundry in 1858, and with a rare brilliance bought old rails cheaply, re-rolled them, and sold them back to the railway at a vast profit. He was not popular with his workforce. Puddler John Hopkins was sentenced to a month in prison for throwing a brick at him after his wages were docked, and an assassination attempt by members of the Iron and Steel Dressers Union failed when the man who drew the short straw lacked courage.

Barningham died in 1882, estranged from his wife, Margaret, and daughter, Mary, and leaving a fortune of £400,000 – more than any individual Pease or Backhouse. This led to the Great Darlington Will Case as Mary successfully fought for her inheritance. With it, she bought Gatherley Castle, near Catterick.

('Memories', *The Northern Echo*, 2010)

29 May

W.G. Grace, aged 25 and at the height of his powers, brought his cricket circus to Feethams. His United South of England XI took on a Darlington District XVIII.

The 'homesters' batted first, all out at 4.45 p.m. for 197. W.G. Grace opened for the South, and the crowd swelled to 3,000. But he was off-colour; J.T. Mewburn, shorthand secretary to Sir Joseph Whitwell Pease MP, dropped him on a single. 'After three-quarters of an hour's play, he struck to square leg, which fell into the hands of Leatham, who retained it,' said the *Echo*. 'This circumstance was very disappointing to the Darlingtonians, who were very anxious to see some tall hitting.'

The next day, when the South's top scorer was caught out by a substitute fielder, an apparently incensed W.G. – a great showman – stormed out of the pavilion and remonstrated with the umpire.

On the final day, Grace's side needed 162 to win. 'At 56, Grace struck a bum-ball, which F. Mewburn handled, and the crowd clapped, imagining that Grace was caught out, and he kept up the illusion by walking away a short distance,' reported the *Echo*. 'Much laughter ensued when he again took his stand at the wicket.' Despite this entertaining piece of cheating, the great man was out a second time without adding to his score and his XI lost by 32.

('Memories', *The Northern Echo*, 2013)

28 March

At 9.50 p.m. on Easter Sunday, John Kilcran, 45, was murdered in Parkgate, near the Cricketers Arms. He was a builder's labourer, married with four children, and was the local secretary of the Hibernian Society, which was involved in an internecine dispute with the local Fenian Society. Rivalry within the Irish community had grown since the first settlers arrived in the 1850s to work in Albert Hill's iron industry.

Indeed, Kilcran had been expected to die in 1873 after an attack in which his hip had been broken. Two years later, seven Irishmen marauded through Skerneside pubs until finding Kilcran and fracturing his skull with a blow so hard it sounded like a pistol had been fired.

Michael Gilligan, a 22-year-old father of two, was charged with his murder. Despite Gilligan's claim that he had been delivering church leaflets at the time of the attack, the jury took fifteen minutes to assess the flimsy evidence and find him guilty. The two Irishmen, James Durkin and James Flynn, who were sentenced to fifteen years for aiding and abetting him, denied that Gilligan had been involved.

Gilligan was hanged on 2 August in Durham's only triple execution. His widow became a recluse, living in the attic of their house at No. 1 Portland Place until her death at the age of 82 in 1935.

('Memories', *The Northern Echo*, 2006)

23 February

The cocoa revolution swept into Darlington with the opening of its first 'cocoa palace' in Melville House, Northgate. Cocoa palaces were the Temperance movement's bid to tempt people away from pubs. 'Since the first Cocoa Palace was opened four or five years ago,' said *The Northern Echo*, 'they have come to be regarded as an important and even necessary institution in most towns.'

The Northgate palace was run by Mr Lockhart, the North East cocoa king, who had twelve palaces on Tyneside. 'The principle on which they are established is even more public than that of the public house, for not only can persons obtain their tea, coffee, cocoa etc upon most reasonable terms, but even those who don't require refreshment are at liberty to go into the rooms and read the papers,' explained the *Echo*.

Unfortunately, Mr Lockhart was too ill to attend the Northgate opening, which was performed by Sir Edmund Backhouse MP. A large cup of cocoa, coffee or tea cost 1*d*; a large spice cake was also 1*d* and a family could buy a 6*d* token for a slap-up refreshment session.

As the cocoa craze caught on, other palaces opened in Prebend Row, Houndgate and Parkgate and Albert Hill – the Nestfield Club and Cocoa Tavern which opened for working men at 5 a.m. The craze, though, lasted barely into the twentieth century.

('Memories', *The Northern Echo*, 1994)

23 October

Thousands witnessed Lady Beatrice Lymington, 19, open the library which bore the name of her late father, Edward Pease. A platform for 400 people had been built outside the library doors, and as she turned the silver key in the lock, she was 'greeted by an outburst of cheering ... by an immense concourse of people'.

The library had been designed by G.G. Hoskins, with the Peases' arms and motto – *pax et spes* (meaning 'peace and hope') – next to a wonderful wise owl in the stonework above the door.

Her ladyship was given a tour by the first librarian, Frank Burgoyne, whose biggest problem in the early days was the large group of illiterate men who gathered on the library steps, waiting for someone to read them the racing tips from the day's newspapers.

After inspecting the facilities, the newly married Lady Lymington and her uncle, Sir Joseph Whitwell Pease, adjourned for speeches and luncheon at the Trevelyan Hotel (now the Imperial). There were more speeches at an evening meeting at the Mechanics Institute in Skinnergate, which was so popular that an overflow meeting was held in the Friends' Meeting House where the speeches were repeated. Doubtless Newton Wallop, Lord Lymington of Portsmouth, who was Beatrice's husband, repeated his best line of the day: 'A library ought to be a club of the best minds of all times.'

('Memories', *The Northern Echo*, 2010)

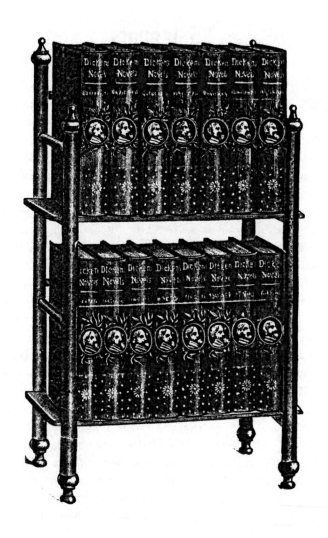

25 January

Willie Smith – known around the world as 'Darlington Smith' – was born in Taylor Street. His father was landlord of the Golden Cock in Tubwell Row where, by the age of 10, Smith was taking on all comers at billiards. He turned professional in 1913 and won the English championship at his first attempt in 1920. He won the world championship in 1921 and 1923, and was greeted at Bank Top station by cheering crowds. He toured the world, and regularly set world records for the biggest break, although his powers started to wane after his favourite cue was snapped during a match in Australia.

In 1933 and 1935 he reached the World Snooker Championship final, where he was beaten by the legendary Joe Davis. On 4 April 1937, he played Horace Lindrum at Alexandra Palace in the world's first televised snooker match, and on 22 January 1955, he watched his opponent, Davis, compile the first 147 break.

He built a chain of snooker halls, including, in 1915, one in Northgate. He died in Leeds in 1982, aged 96. Leading snooker commentator Clive Everton said: 'There is no doubt that he was one of the all-time greats. He played the billiards of the common man, and he was always identified with the common man. He was a terrific character and had a tremendous sense of humour.'

('Memories', *The Northern Echo*, 2002)

1 July

Bank Top station opened without any ceremony. 'Even yet the finishing touches are to be given but the building is sufficiently near completion to show that it is among the largest and most notable of its kind in the country,' said *The Northern Echo* on the station's first day of operation.

It was really an accidental station, as North Road, on the 1825 Stockton and Darlington Railway, was regarded as the town's main station, so when the mainline opened in 1841, an unattractive shed was provided for its passengers. Queen Victoria stopped there on 28 September 1849 and was surprised that the birthplace of the railways could offer nothing fancier.

Bank Top is a back-to-front station. The chief architect of the North Eastern Railway, William Bell, and the engineer-in-chief, Thomas Harrison, started work in early 1885 on an 'island' station, with lines running on either side of the railway buildings. They built a grand entrance, topped by an 80ft clock tower, in the newly created Victoria Road, and excavated liftshafts to connect passengers with the island. But the railway directors decided that the cost of manning the lifts twenty-four hours a day was too expensive. So the lifts were never installed, and instead passengers were encouraged to forsake the grand main entrance and instead use the Parkgate goods entrance, where a ramp runs up onto the island.

('Memories', *The Northern Echo*, 2012)

28 January

At 9.40 p.m., the fire brigade based under the Covered Market received 'telephonic communication' that the North of England School Furnishing Company in East Mount Road was ablaze. A bell in the clock tower was rung to summon the firemen, but it also alerted the townspeople so that when the firemen reached the blaze at 10 p.m., 3,000 spectators were present – many of them sheltering from the heat beneath the workshop's west wall. 'Just after half-past ten o'clock, a flash of light was observed ... and then followed a report like that of a piece of ordnance,' said *The Northern Echo*. 'Almost simultaneously, the gable end of the wall blew out and TONS OF BRICKS FELL ON THE PEOPLE BELOW.'

Two men were pulled from the rubble, dead. 'Their heads and faces were totally unrecognisable, and their trunks had been beaten into a horrible misshapen mess,' said the paper. 'Then came young boys with heads covered with blood and dangling limbs.' George Carter, 41, was rushed to hospital to have his leg amputated; he survived, and was one of the fifteen seriously injured.

Lionel Stainsby, 18, was rushed for emergency trepanning – having his skull sawn open – but he became one of five fatalities. At their inquests at the Railway Tavern, the coroner ordered that a runner, not the town bell, should in future be used to summon firemen.

('Memories', *The Northern Echo*, 2002)

9 October

'Appalling powder explosion at Darlington', screamed the headline in *The Northern Echo*.

> Houses in Skinnergate, High Row and Blackwellgate rocked as if about to fall, while glass clattered and burst from almost every window. Immediately the air was filled with a cloud of smoke, from which descended a veritable hail of mortar, glass, wood, iron and pulverised brickwork. All around in the streets and lanes this fell, injuring some people and frightening many more.

Joseph Forestall Smythe was the only gunmaker between York and Newcastle. Behind his shop at No. 13 Blackwellgate, 370,000 cartridges were loaded each year – until his loading room exploded, reducing the Mechanics Yard area to matchsticks.

His apprentice, Thomas Howe, 14, was 'discovered lying with a heavy bench vice jammed hard against his disfigured face and with his arms crushed under him,' reported the *Darlington and Stockton Times*. 'His mangled form' was stretchered through the streets to Russell Street Hospital where he died.

A London inspector found 'a portion of a toy pistol, an empty cigarette case and an obsolete military nipple key' in Howe's pockets and blamed the explosion on 'some boyish experiment'. Modern thinking is that the building's wooden frame soaked up powder dust like a sponge until, saturated, it was ignited by a spark from a hobnail boot.

('Memories', *The Northern Echo*, 2004)

8 November

Squire Cocks died, aged 89 and unmarried, after a lifetime of generosity – of both money and affections. Henry Andrew William Cocks was the last of the Killinghall and Pemberton families, which had ruled Middleton St George for six centuries. He built the village's first ironworks, and he donated money to schools and churches.

In his will, he left £1,000 each to 'my two reputed sons' Charles and Arthur Robinson, plus a further £1,000 to 'my reputed son' Frederick Robinson, as long as he didn't fall into debt. Another £1,000 was left to 'my reputed son, Henry Wilkinson, of Middleton One Row, postmaster'.

Squire Cocks left £2,000 each to 'my three reputed daughters' Harrietta, Louisa and Patience Graham, 'children of my friend, the late Margaret Ann Graham of Middleton One Row'.

Wilmot Warmington, 'son of Mrs Sarah Warmington of Wolverhampton', inherited another £500. How Mrs Warmington warmed the cockles of Squire Cocks' heart is unknown.

He also left £200 to his housekeeper Alice Slater 'as an acknowledgement of her kindness and attention to me'.

Another £200 bequest was to the Wesleyan chapel in Middleton One Row, the construction of which he had funded in 1872 with identical houses on either side of it. It is said these matching homes accommodated his most accommodating mistresses: Mistress Robinson on one side and Mistress Graham on the other.

('Memories', *The Northern Echo*, 2004)

24 June

Nazrulla Khan, the Shahzada of Afghanistan, was met by a 100-man guard of honour at Bank Top station. Along with 100,000 others, including the Duke and Duchess of York, he was visiting the week-long Royal Agricultural Society show at Hummersknott.

The Shahzada, the 20-year-old heir to the Afghan throne, the Kotwal of Kabul and the Nakim Bashi stayed at Polam Hall, but as it had recently been turned into a girls' school, incense had to be burned throughout to remove the 'female pollution'.

The Shahzada came with cases of oranges, sacks of rice and live sheep and chickens, which were slaughtered and cooked on a specially-constructed stove – it is said that you can still see the scorch marks on the wooden floor beneath the carpet in Polam library.

The next morning, as the Shahzada departed, he breezily inquired if he could buy Polam. At Hummersknott, he strolled around the butter-making and poultry-dressing displays, and then returned with his colourful entourage to Bank Top for the evening train to London. 'Some were wearing turbans and others caps of astrachan,' said the *Echo*. 'One had a bright green cloth edged with red lovingly tucked under his arm; another carried a prosaic portmanteau; a third had a mysterious bundle enclosed in a white cloth and a fourth, umbrella in hand, had a few gay blossoms beneath his fingers.'

('Memories', *The Northern Echo*, 2004)

22 June

Darlington revived its traditional royal celebration of a public ox roast for Queen Victoria's diamond jubilee. 'Residents near the Market Place look forward with considerable misgiving to this ceremony, owing to the smell of burnt flesh and coke smoke,' said the *Darlington and Stockton Times*.

A 60-stone ox was hoisted by a large crane from Cleveland Bridge onto a spit made by Darlington Forge. It had salt from Messrs Mawson, Swan & Morgan of Newcastle rubbed into it and was roasted for twenty-four hours by six braziers lent by the North Eastern Railway, while the Gravy Making Society did its work. A bathful of fat was available for those who wanted dripping.

It was such a success that another ox was roasted on 22 August 1902, for the coronation of Edward VII, and fed 2,000 people. But the misgivings grew, as demonstrated by this letter to the *Darlington and Stockton Times* from an anonymous poet:

This ox of sterling value will not hunger pangs avail,
When charred and marred and shrivelled from head to tail.

A third ox was roasted in 1911 for George V's coronation. 'It would be impossible to roast an ox better,' concluded the secretary of the Ox Roasting Committee, and many homes still contain one of the 2,724 commemorative plates (cost: 5*s* 9*d* a dozen) upon which he handed out the sandwiches.

('Memories', *The Northern Echo*, 2012)

30 December

On this day, Sir Henry Havelock-Allan of Blackwell Grange was murdered in the Khyber Pass. He had been awarded the Victoria Cross during the Indian Mutiny of 1857, and had fought around the world for the Empire until, in 1880, he inherited the Blackwell estate. From 1874 to 1881, he was MP for Sunderland, and then he represented south-east Durham. He applied warlike tactics to the House of Commons: he so disliked what one Irish MP was saying that he went over and sat on him.

During the Parliamentary recess of 1897, Sir Henry, aged 67, went out to study the Indian Army, and died in a botched kidnap attempt in the Khyber Pass.

A companion recalled:

> We found him lying in the dried up bed of a rocky nullah (a ravine), under the shade of a solitary tree whose gnarled roots were exposed. On one of these he apparently, when wounded, had seated himself until, weakened by the loss of blood, he rolled down, two or three feet, into the nullah below … His murderers had stripped him of all but his underclothing, but they had in no way mutilated his body, and as he lay there stretched out on his back, one was struck by the calm of his countenance. His moustaches were still waxed and, but for the paleness, one could almost have imagined him asleep.

('Memories', *The Northern Echo*, 1993)

20 January

A telegram from Venezuela reached the family of the British Vice-Consul, James Lyall, in Vane Terrace, Darlington. It said his murderer had been sentenced to eleven years' penal servitude, thus ending a diplomatic incident that had seen a British warship sent up the Orinoco River in South America.

James, a former pupil of Darlington Grammar School, became the British Vice-Consul in the town of Ciudad Bolivar, Venezuela, in October 1898. In a long letter home, he told how he had been paddled up the Orinoco by Native Indians wearing nothing but loincloths, and how he was dining on turtles' eggs and roast monkey. But he concluded: 'There is not a great deal of social life, families and friends being so disorganised by the revolutions which take place almost annually.'

In the following February's revolution, James was 'fatally stabbed to the body by a drunken villain', dying in the arms of the British consul, Mr C.H. de Lomas, who said in his telegram that 'the motive for the deed seemed to be political animosity'.

When the Venezuelan Government dragged its heels about arresting the assassin and paying compensation, the British Foreign Office sailed HMS *Alert* up the Orinoco. In response, the Venezuelans sent a telegram declaring that an unnamed murderer had been imprisoned – although no compensation was ever paid.

('Memories', *The Northern Echo*, 2001)

13 April

Daniel Crosthwaite became the first person to be cremated in Darlington – a year before cremation was legalised in Britain.

The Darlington Cremation Society formed in March 1890 when cremation was controversial – 'it is neither reasonable, decent nor reverent and we do not want such a pagan practice in our midst', a meeting of anti-cremationists in Northgate was told in 1892.

The society raised £1,000 to build a small chapel and coke-fired incinerator in West Cemetery, and tested it on 19 March 1901. 'It was intended to get the dead body of a sheep but this couldn't be arranged, so portions of a horse were placed in the coffin which, by the way, was more massive than usual,' said the *Darlington and Stockton Times*. 'The chamber was heated to 1,800 Fahrenheit degrees and the reduction of the coffin and its contents was carried out with the reasonable expedition anticipated.'

Mr Crosthwaite was a pro-cremation brewer from Saltburn. On 13 April, his body arrived at Bank Top on the 3.30 p.m. train. It processed through the town on a brewer's dray, watched by a considerable crowd, and its cremation took an hour and forty minutes. It was judged a great success.

On 1 July 1904, railway guard Mr W. Banks became the first Darlingtonian to be cremated. Until 1930, Darlington had the only crematorium between the rivers Tweed and Humber.

('Memories', *The Northern Echo*, 2001)

31 December

Reviewing the year in which the fortunes of the Pease family had collapsed, Sir Joseph Whitwell Pease wrote in his diary: 'We wound up the law suit with Lord and Lady Portsmouth in which we all felt we were most iniquitously robbed ...'

He had taken in Lady Beatrice Portsmouth, his niece, as a 14-year-old orphan. Aged 18, she had fallen for Lord Porstmouth – then known as Lord Lymington, real name Newton Wallop – who was ten years her elder, and whom Sir Joseph described as a 'fortune hunter'. For fifteen years, Lord Portsmouth pursued Sir Joseph for Beatrice's inheritance. After protracted High Court cases – in which the judge devastatingly described Sir Joseph as an 'unsatisfactory witness' – the Peases had been ordered to pay £302,000 (about £30 million today).

Unfortunately, Sir Joseph could not afford this, so he had to rapidly sell his mansion and all his assets. He was only saved from bankruptcy by his Quaker banking friends.

He blamed the Portsmouths for his downfall. He concluded his 1901 diary: 'After having found her a home till marriage ... after having done all I could through all the bad times of the coal trade ... they charged us with fraud ... and (my brother) Arthur's estate and mine were defrauded ... Such is gratitude and love.'

He died a broken man two years later.

('Memories', *The Northern Echo*, 2010)

18 August

The last of Darlington's horse-drawn trams ran on this day. The town's first horse-drawn tram system had collapsed acrimoniously after three years in 1865, but in 1880, the Stockton and Darlington Steam Tramway Company opened a new system, using twelve cars – some double-decker – on three routes radiating from the Market Place to the North Road Works, Cockerton and Bank Top station. However, the horses had to be severely whipped to encourage them to pull the 5-ton cars up the slight inclines of Woodland Road and Northgate (the poor animals were also expected to turn out and pull the town's fire engine when an emergency arose).

The company, which had its depot in Woodland Road near Portland Place, was regularly in financial difficulties. In 1885, it dropped the Bank Top route; in 1890 it went into liquidation, and in 1896 it was bought by the Imperial Tramways Company of Bristol, which intended to electrify it.

But in 1900, Darlington Corporation opened a new power station on Haughton Road and decided it would like to run an electric tramway. It bought Imperial out for £7,600 in January 1902, and on 17 August 1903, it made thirty-five horses and their drivers redundant, with the last horse-drawn tram running the following day. The electric tramway was opened on 1 June 1904.

('Memories', *The Northern Echo*, 1994)

5 August

Earl Frederick Roberts, 1st Baron of Kandahar in Afghanistan and the first Freeman of the Borough of Darlington, unveiled the South African War Memorial in St Cuthbert's churchyard.

Roberts was British commander-in-chief at the end of the Boer War in South Africa and in 1904 had been invited to inspect the railway bridge that Darlington's Cleveland Bridge was constructing over the River Zambezi near the Victoria Falls. Company director William Pease, of Mowden Hall, took Lord Roberts across the terrifying gorge in a cage suspended from a steel rope. Halfway across, Pease stopped the cage so that Roberts could see how the two halves of the bridge would be bolted together. As they swung there 250ft from safety, Pease jokingly threatened to throw Roberts 420ft into the Zambezi – unless he came to Darlington to unveil the war memorial. Which he did.

The *Darlington and Stockton Times* reported:

> The scene, with Earl Roberts in his field marshal's uniform, his breast covered in medals and orders, the members of the corporation in their robes, the volunteers in their uniforms, the members of the fire brigade, and spectators on the grandstands, the venerable church tower, roofs and windows, and filling the streets as far as the eye could reach, and the memorial as the central point, was one of the most impressive ever beheld in Darlington.

('Memories', *The Northern Echo*, 2012)

13 September

'Build a bridge across the River Zambezi where the trains, as they pass, will catch the spray of the Victoria Falls,' instructed magnate Cecil Rhodes, and the men of Darlington did, their extraordinary construction being opened by Professor George Darwin, the son of Charles, on this day.

Because of the heat of the African sun, the bridge was designed to expand and lift on giant hinged bearings bolted into the sides of the 820ft-wide gorge.

The bridge was built in sections in Darlington by Cleveland Bridge, a company formed in 1877 by Albert Hill steelworkers on the strawberry patch of Polam Hall in Smithfield Road. On 5 March 1904, they despatched the 1,868-ton segments by train to Middlesbrough from where they sailed to Africa. With the pieces went '20 skilled mechanics or erectors' who, for the next year, lived in huts on the south bank of the Zambezi, according to *The Northern Echo*. They bolted their bits together until the two sides of the bridge met in the middle on the evening of 31 March 1905. But they were 1¾ inches out. They returned to their huts in disappointment, but during the cool night their steel contracted, and at 7 a.m. next morning, it fitted perfectly.

Local tribal chief Mukuni explained how this graceful arch could hang 420ft above the river: 'It is held up by the finger of the white man's god.'

('Memories', *The Northern Echo*, 2012)

6 August

The silence of a Quaker wedding service in the Friends Meeting House, Skinnergate, was drowned out by a thunderstorm which washed out the reception. 'Life can't be all happiness,' said the bride, Katherine Maria Pease, as she married Australian explorer-archaeologist, William Scoresby Routledge, and embarked on an extraordinary voyage.

Katherine was the grand-daughter of Joseph Pease, and the daughter of Gurney – her line of the family was bedevilled by mental illness. She also suffered a stultifying childhood, from which her husband – although they probably never loved one another – was her escape. To him, her £20,000 dowry was a means of funding travel.

First they spent two years exploring the tribal customs of East Africa. Then, on 28 March 1914, they landed on Easter Island, in the Pacific Ocean, 1,350 miles from its nearest neighbour. Katherine stayed for sixteen months, the first archaeologist to record the supersize statues and the folklore of their people.

She returned to astonishment – women just didn't do this sort of thing. Even George V was interested in what she had to say about the most remote part of his empire.

Sadly, she could never repeat this success, and she sank into a reclusiveness in London populated by her family's ghosts. She died in a lunatic asylum in Sussex on 13 December 1935.

('Memories', *The Northern Echo*, 2011, and van Tilburg)

12 December

An 'exceptional consignment' was transported from Darlington Forge on Albert Hill to the shearlegs at the Union Dock, West Hartlepool. It was the cast steel stern frame, rudder and brackets 'which have been manufactured for the *Titanic*, one of the two mammoth steamships for the White Star Line which are now being built at Harland and Wolff's shipyard at Belfast', said *The Northern Echo*. 'They rank as by far and away the largest castings ever made in connection with marine engineering work.'

The forge had been building supersize pieces for ocean-going liners since 1897, including for Cunard's famous Blue Riband winners, the *Lusitania* and the *Mauretania*. But the 280-ton metalwork for the *Titanic* was so wide that the tracks on either side of the special train had to be empty of traffic, and men walked alongside, apparently with the instruction to throw themselves beneath a piece if it slipped off its truck (in reality, they were there to remove telegraph poles and dismantle bridges as the enormous load went past)..

According to the *Echo*: 'The stern frame special left Darlington at eight o'clock and travelling at a speed never exceeding a brisk walking pace, safely arrived at the shipping point at West Hartlepool, a distance of about 25 miles, shortly before dusk.'

From there, it was loaded onto a steamship called *Glendun* and sailed to Belfast. Now, of course, it lies 350 miles south east of Newfoundland, 12,000ft at the bottom of the Atlantic Ocean.

('Memories', *The Northern Echo*, 2012)

20 August

Mary Lawson was born at No. 58, Pease Street, off Yarm Road. She became a West End star who, for eight months, was engaged to Fred Perry – one of Britain's greatest sports stars.

She started singing for injured soldiers when she was 5, and was known as 'the Scala Pet', entertaining in the Eldon Street cinema as the projectionist changed the reel. At 12, she left school and toured in a musical comedy called *Sunshine Sally*. As her mother had died when she was 3, and her father was a North Eastern Railway crane driver, she was chaperoned by her elder sister, Dora.

In London's West End in 1925, she was paired with an up-and-coming dancer called Max Wall. Gracie Fields championed her, and she made 650 consecutive appearances, establishing herself as 'a most alluring little dunce', in White Horse Inn at the London Coliseum.

Later, Mary moved into films. On the set of *Falling in Love* in 1934, she fell in love with Wimbledon winner Fred Perry. When they became engaged, they were the celebrity couple of the moment – until Mary said: 'Publicity has killed our romance.'

In 1937, she married film producer Francis W.L.C. Beaumont, but the pair were killed in a German air raid on Liverpool on 4 May 1941. 'Little Mary Lawson … the petite, retrousee-nosed, earnest North of England girl', as she was described in a stage magazine, was only 31.

('Memories', *The Northern Echo*, 2010)

1 October

Florence Trusler, 18, set a world record in Darlington's Kendrew Street baths by swimming 12 miles and 46¾ yards non-stop, in nine hours and twenty minutes. 'Miss Trusler is, in short, something in the nature of a phenomenon,' said *The Northern Echo*.

Florrie announced herself in 1909 by diving into the baths without any training and swimming 10 miles in seven hours, forty-three minutes and twenty-eight seconds. The next year, having swum in the Thames, she set her world record, sometimes swimming on her back, sometimes doing breaststroke. While in the water, she consumed three bananas, three spoonfuls of honey and three small pieces of bread and cheese, and was only forced from the water by a knee strain.

'Physically, she was almost as fresh and strong as when she entered the water, in proof of which Miss Trusler covered her last length in thirty-one seconds – five seconds better than when she won the Darlington championship,' noted the *Echo*. 'She is a non-flesh eater, never has more than two meals a day, and on the morning of her most recent performance had at six o'clock a breakfast of two boiled eggs and a little brown bread. Afterwards, she ate two apples and a little bread and cheese, and drank a glass of milk.'

Florrie married and moved to Reeth where she died in 1984, aged 92.

('Memories', *The Northern Echo*, 2002)

25 April

'La Milo, whose marvellously clever representations of classical statuary provoked such a storm of criticism a year or two ago is the great attraction this week,' said *The Northern Echo* of the star turn at the New Hippodrome and Palace Theatre of Varieties (now the Civic Theatre).

La Milo was a voluptuous Australian actress called Pansy Montague. She was 'the female form displayed in all its essential detail', whose living statuary act caused outrage when she arrived in Britain in 1906. She would pour her curves into a tight pink leotard or, if she was feeling brave, strip naked and cover them with white enamel paint. Then she would go on stage and impersonate 'with marvellous fidelity and skill … some of the best known works of sculptural art'.

Using 'imperceptible breathing' so that no part of her moved, the 'pose plastique performer' stood stock still impersonating famous statues, including the Venus de Milo. 'The Modern Milo', though, clearly had two arms, unlike the statue in the Louvre – but the men in the audience were looking at her other charms …

'The storm which burst over her head when first she entered upon her task of presenting to the public her studies in breathing marble of the statues of antiquity has largely died away, and now her performance is acclaimed as beautifully artistic,' concluded the *Echo*.

('Memories', *The Northern Echo*, 2009)

11 December

George Gordon Hoskins died at his home of Thornbeck Hill, off Coniscliffe Road. 'He has distinguished himself by his great architectural genius, abundant evidence of which is manifest in his imposing buildings,' said the mayor. 'He has left many things behind him to keep his memory fresh.'

In fact, G.G. Hoskins created the face of Victorian Darlington. His quirkily grand style and unique terracotta touch was known as 'Hoskinian Gothic', and it gained for Darlington the nickname of 'the Athens of the North'. Among his achievements are Elm Ridge (1865), Queen Elizabeth Sixth Form College (1875), Crown Street (1879–82), the Pease Public Library (1884), King's Head Hotel (1890) and the Technical College (1894).

He grew up in Burton-on-Trent in the shadow of an extravagant hilltop mock Gothic folly that had ruined his grandfather. In 1861, Manchester architect Alfred Waterhouse sent Hoskins to Hurworth to be clerk of works on Pilmore Hall – now Rockliffe Hall – that Waterhouse was building for banker Alfred Backhouse. This was the start Hoskins needed, and the young George became Backhouses' banks' in-house architect, designing branches including Bishop Auckland and Barnard Castle.

His magnum opus, though, is Middlesbrough Town Hall. It is a £130,000 masterpiece from its crypt to its belfry, which was opened by the future King Edward VII in 1889, although his best building is surely Darlington's opulent King's Head Hotel.

('Memories', *The Northern Echo*, 2008)

15 April

The most famous British person among the 1,500 casualties of the *Titanic* disaster was W.T. Stead, the second editor of *The Northern Echo*.

Stead was just 21 and working as a clerk on Newcastle's Quayside in 1871 when he was offered the editor's chair, and he spent the next decade blowing the Liberal trumpet, campaigning against social injustices and sensationalising the story of the West Auckland mass murderer, Mary Ann Cotton.

In 1877, he organised scores of 'atrocity meetings' in which ordinary people demanded that the Conservative government should stop the Ottoman Empire slaughtering its Bulgarian subjects – a campaign that led directly to W.E. Gladstone's Liberal Party winning the 1880 General Election. Gladstone rewarded Stead by promoting him to the *Pall Mall Gazette* in London, where he triumphantly campaigned against the trade in young girls in the capital's brothels.

Stead had become fascinated with spiritualism while in Darlington, and in 1912 he was sailing on the *Titanic* to New York to address a spiritualist peace conference with the US president, William Taft. He was in cabin C89 when the iceberg struck and he was last seen, with the deck listing perilously, asking the ship's orchestra to play his favourite hymn, 'Nearer My God to Thee'.

The cheese press to which he used to tether his pony is now a memorial dedicated to him outside Darlington library.

('Memories', *The Northern Echo*, 2012)

4 July

Goalkeeper R.G. Brebner became the first – and possibly only – Darlington-born person to win an Olympic gold medal. He attended Darlington Grammar School and later became a dentist, filling cavities in his practice in Coniscliffe Road, but he also filled in between the sticks for Darlington FC as an amateur goalkeeper. In 1910, he was man of the match as the Quakers humbled First Division Sheffield United – 'rarely before could such a masterly exhibition of goalkeeping have been seen at Bramall Lane', declared the *Echo* – during their great FA Cup. The following season, he turned out for Queen's Park Rangers and Huddersfield Town.

He played in all three of Great Britain's matches at the 1912 Stockholm Olympics, including the 4–2 win over Denmark in the final.

However, about two months after winning his gold medal, he was injured – possibly when diving at the feet of an opponent – while playing for Leicester Fosse against Wolverhampton Wanderers, and never recovered. He died eighteen months later, aged 33. 'He was undoubtedly one of the most capable amateur goalkeepers in the country, and he attained practically all the honours that come to an amateur, although his ambition to be selected in a representative game for all England was never realised,' said his obituary in the *Darlington and Stockton Times*. He is buried in West Cemetery.

('Memories', *The Northern Echo*, 2012)

18 September

The evening's *Northern Despatch* reported the deaths of Private Albert Peart, 29, a Co-op grocer from Wales Street, and of Lieutenant Ronald Pike Pease, 19, of Hummersknott, the son of the local MP. Peart and Pease had died on the same day in the same battle: Flers-Courcelette, the first tank engagement.

The paper also contained news of the deaths of Captain David Henderson, 27, the son of Arthur Henderson, the former Mayor of Darlington who had just become the first Labour representative ever to sit in the Cabinet, and of Lieutenant Raymond Asquith, 37, the son of the prime minister H.H. Asquith.

It also included the story of Captain Hugh Wilson, 38, of Langholm Crescent, a veteran of the Boer War. Five days before Flers-Courcelette, he and two officers had drawn straws to see who would go over the top first. Captain Wilson had drawn the shortest, and had immediately been shot through the heart.

He was buried in the same cemetery as Captain Thomas Rowlandson, 36, of Newton Morrell, near Barton, who had also died at Flers-Courcelette. The paper noted that Charterhouse- and Cambridge-educated Rowlandson had played for Corinthian FC and had captained 'an English team' on a tour of South Africa. It said he died racing his men across no-man's-land towards the German trenches, armed only with a walking stick.

('Memories', *The Northern Echo*, 2012)

23 April

St George's Day: the day Lieutenant-Commander George Bradford was born in 1887, and the day he died winning the Victoria Cross in 1918.

George grew up at Morton Palms Farm, on Darlington's eastern edge. His father insisted he walk 4 miles into school because it was good for his character. When George was 11, the family moved into Milbank Road and he attended the grammar school.

He joined the Royal Navy in 1904, and had a quiet war until he volunteered to scuttle concrete-filled ships in Zeebrugge harbour to stop U-boats sneaking out and attacking British shipping. But the sea was too rough for his assault ship, *Iris II*, to land. Huge waves kept crashing it against the harbour wall.

Under heavy fire, George climbed to the top of the on-board crane, waited until the *Iris II* rose on a wave and then jumped onto the harbour wall, securing an anchor-hold so his men could follow him ashore.

But as he landed, every German gunner turned on him. He was riddled with bullets and his body fell into the sea. 'His action was one of absolute self-sacrifice,' said his VC citation.

His younger brother, Brigadier-General Roland Boys Bradford, had been awarded a posthumous VC on 30 November 1917 – the only brothers to win the nation's highest bravery honour in the First World War.

('Memories', *The Northern Echo*, 2013)

1 August

A 'great novelty angling contest' was the highlight of the second annual gala held on the South Park boating lake. The contest pitted Dr Begg, president of the Bath Angling Association and England's champion angler, against 'the human salmon' – Middlesbrough's legendary swimmer Jack Hatfield, who had won three medals at the 1912 Olympics.

The lake opposite Blackwell Grange had opened in 1925, having been dug out by unemployed men, and canvas sheets were stretched around its fencing to prevent the thousands of spectators from seeing the terrifically exciting contest without paying.

'Hatfield undertook to have a line similar to that used for salmon fishing tied around his waist and connected to the rod in the hands of Dr Begg, 74, and to defy the efforts of the angler to land the "catch",' reported *The Northern Echo*.

The contest began: the human salmon thrashed around in the water while the champion angler battled with his tackle on the bank. 'The novel contest lasted for 17½ minutes when it had a rather unfortunate ending,' reported the *Echo*. 'Hatfield proved too powerful for the fisherman and in the end Dr Begg collapsed from exhaustion following a strenuous struggle between him and the fish … He had to receive attention from officials who brought him round with towels … To mark his victory, Hatfield received a gold enamel medal.'

('Memories', *The Northern Echo*, 2006)

4 September

Alderman William Edwin Pease, who doubled as Darlington's mayor and MP, opened the Cockerbeck Valley Park – now known as the Denes.

After the Peases vacated their mansions of Pierremont and Brinkburn at the start of the twentieth century, the project to turn their steeply sided valley into a public park was held up by the First World War. The war was followed by an even more protracted battle with allotment holders, who had created piggeries and hen runs by the beck.

The westernmost dene, Brinkburn, was opened to the public on 11 September 1923, but the battle – 'rather a violent one', remembered a councillor – with the allotment holders was not settled by the Ministry of Agriculture in London until mid-1924. Unemployed men were put to work converting the allotments, planting more than 10,000 trees and shrubs and laying 1½ miles of path.

About 2,000 people watched Alderman Pease perform the opening ceremony at the Salisbury Terrace entrance. 'Darlington's latest lung is the Cockerbeck Valley Park, a mass of green slopes and shrubberies to the extent of 23 acres through which flows, like a silver ribbon, the charming beck,' said the *Evening Despatch*. 'The new park is very beautiful and will be a source of pleasure and health to children and adults who reside in its neighbourhood.'

(Lloyd: *A History of the Denes of Darlington*)

17 November

Anna Pavlova, the Russian ballerina who was the greatest superstar of her day, danced at the New Hippodrome and Palace Theatre of Varieties – now the Civic Theatre. Her booking was a coup for the Italian impresario Signor Rino Pepi, who founded the theatre, and died on the same day.

Pepi was born in Florence in 1872 and became the finest quick-change artiste in all Europe. In 1898, he topped the bill in London's West End and then, encouraged by his wife Mary, Countess de Rossetti, he went into theatre management. He operated a string of music halls from Blackpool to Middlesbrough, although those in Barrow and Darlington, which he opened on 2 September 1907, were the most enduring.

All Darlington turned out to watch Pavlova process from the station to the theatre, but only the wealthiest could see her perform (dress circle tickets were 10s 6d). Tragically, Pepi wasn't among them. Several hours after she closed with her *pièce de theatre* – the dying swan from Saint Saen's Carnival of the Animals – Pepi died of cancer of the left lung at his home in Tower Road. He was 55.

He was buried alongside his countess in Barrow, although his ghost still haunts dressing room No. 5 – once his one-bedroom apartment – and it appears in the royal box stage right a second before curtain up.

('Memories', *The Northern Echo*, 2006)

4 June

The Sir E.D. Walker Homes – 'a haven of eventide' and 'a picture of paradise for old folk' – were opened on Coniscliffe Road by the Marchioness of Aberdeen and Temair.

Sir E.D. – Edward Daniel – was born into a Brighton seafaring family in 1844 and came north when his coastguard father was posted to Redcar. E.D., as he was known, worked as a clerk for the North Eastern Railway until he set up his own business, managing station newsstands and advertising hoardings. He became known as 'the W.H. Smith of the North', diversifying from kiosks into refreshment rooms, and then into corner shops.

A keen cricketer and rose-grower, he owned *The Northern Echo* and was twice mayor. 'The Grand Old Man' of Darlington died in May 1919, and instructed that his estate be used to provide comfortable homes for the aged working-class poor.

His model village had thirty-eight single-storey apartments, houses for a superintendent and a nurse, plus 'an airy, lightsome and healthful' communal hall. There were 180 applications for the seventy-two places, and among the first residents were Mr and Mrs Samuel Evison, aged 67 and 68, who were overjoyed at the electric lights and 'plentiful and beautiful' hot water. Referring to the prospect of the workhouse, Mrs Evison said: 'I thank God and Sir Edward Walker that I am at this end of the town – and not at the other.'

('Memories', *The Northern Echo*, 2013)

27 June

The Darlington rail disaster killed twenty-five people and injured forty-nine when, at 11.20 p.m., a parcels train, which had started in Newcastle and was bound for York, emerged from the southern end of Bank Top station. Its driver, R.J. Bell, was on his first journey to Darlington and, as he had previously only worked in the Newcastle yard, had no knowledge of mainline signals. Believing he 'had the boards', he slipped past signals that were at danger and came to a halt with his train straddling the mainline. Then he saw the headlights of an approaching excursion train, returning at 45mph from Scarborough to Newcastle.

The passenger train ripped through the parcels train, dragging it 60 yards up the track. The impact caused the eleven passenger coaches to telescope, with the undercarriage of the third coach being torn through the second coach in which eighteen members of Hetton-le-Hole Mothers' Union were sitting. 'The rescuers found great difficulty in extricating people from the wrecked carriages,' reported the *Echo*. 'Shrill cries and moans came every few seconds from the wreckage.'

By 4 a.m., Hetton was in mourning: of the Mothers' Union party, only three survived, including Dorothea Smith, the wife of the vicar who conducted fifteen funerals that weekend.

The inquiry primarily blamed Driver Bell, but also criticised the London North Eastern Railway's driver training.

('Memories', *The Northern Echo*, 1996)

3 July

A crowd of about 500 cheered loudly as Alfonso XIII, the King of Spain, stepped from the 10.03 p.m. train onto Bank Top platform. A further 500 were noisily awaiting him at the Imperial Hotel, in Grange Road. 'As he stepped out of his car and heard the cheering, he took off his hat and waved a greeting to the crowd,' reported *The Northern Echo*. 'A woman standing near the door shouted "cheerio", and very softly the king answered: "Same to you".'

The next morning, hundreds lined the streets and Spanish flags flew from the chimneys as he was driven to Darlington Forge, on Albert Hill, for a mystery visit. The *Echo* declared that 'no one supposes that King Alfonso is going to spend seven hours in the works for the good of his health'.

He spent all day apparently fascinated by a new casting process devised by a French engineer, Sgr Bernardini. 'The king talked fluently in English in a slightly foreign accent, and showed an extensive knowledge of metallurgical processes,' said the paper. He was 'loath to leave', but the 5.30 p.m. express was waiting for him. The *Echo* continued: 'He was given a memento of his visit in the shape of a steel ashtray cast from the steel which he had seen in liquid form passing from the converter in the small casting shop.'

('Memories', *The Northern Echo*, 2013)

23 December

A raffle with the top prize of a new house was drawn. It was organised to raise money for the Memorial Hospital by the local Rotary Club, whose members had given the land in Latimer Street, designed and built the house, and then sold the tickets.

'All the counterfoils – about 11,000 of them – were rolled up and placed in a bed tick and Mrs L. Richmond, of Ipswich, drew out 440,' reported the *Echo*. A bed tick was a large bag for keeping bedding in, but Mrs Richmond's involvement is unexplained.

The paper continued: 'She then made a second draw of 44, and in turn reduced these to five. From these, three were selected, and the draw proper then made.' B1579 was unrolled. On the back, it said: 'RG Suggett, Humor Villa, Eastbourne Road, Darlington.'

The *Echo* explained: 'Mr Suggett is well known, not only in Eastbourne – the ward he represents on the town council – but all over the town and in the dales. He has been a member of the council for eight years, and in various committees has rendered valuable service.' Rotary, comprised of many councillors, had contrived to give its star prize to a councillor.

Councillor Suggett, for his part, said: 'It is a very pleasant surprise. It is the first time I have ever won anything in a draw.'

('Memories', *The Northern Echo*, 2007)

21 October

The Nignog Club for children made its debut in *The Northern Echo*. It was run by Uncle Mac (Derek McCullogh, who also hosted the BBC's Children's Hour on the wireless) and Uncle Ernest (Ernest Noble, a Darlington artist who drew the cartoons). It was named after Nig and Nog, who were 'two little imps who live in the Land of the Moon, their chief occupation to keep the Man in the Moon awake'. 'Nig' and 'nog' was also County Durham vernacular for 'boy' and 'girl'.

Three months later, the club welcomed its 50,000th member – an expansion so rapid that the factory producing the blue-and-white enamel Nignog badges couldn't keep up. A Nignog troupe toured village halls putting on entertainment shows, and all Nignogs raised funds to send less fortunate children to Cober Hill guest house near Scarborough. On 6 May 1933, Prince George, the Duke of Kent, visited the 400 children the Nignogs had sent to convalesce on the clifftops, and he was enrolled as an honorary Nignog.

However, on 1 September 1939, Uncle David – who had taken over the club in 1936 – suddenly appeared Nignogless in the paper, with just his 'Children's Corner'. The next day, both he and his 'Children's Corner' disappeared without explanation and on 3 September, the Second World War broke out. Nig and Nog never returned.

(Lloyd: *Attacking the Devil*)

13 December

Arthur Wharton, the first black professional footballer, died on this day. Born in Ghana in 1865, his wealthy parents sent him to a nonconformist boarding school in Milbank Road, Darlington, when he was 19. In May 1885, he appeared at a Feethams sports day, and won the 100 yards despite ducking beneath the finishing tape.

He joined Darlington FC and 'earned fame as a brilliant goalkeeper'. The *Echo* noted: 'He could fist a ball almost as far as a man could kick it.' He could also swing from the crossbar and catch the ball between his legs. In July 1886, Wharton astounded the 2,000-strong crowd at the Amateur Athletics Association championships at Stamford Bridge by winning the 100 yards in ten seconds exactly – the first time in the world this had been reliably recorded.

Now big box office, he made guest appearances for many athletics and football clubs, including the Quakers, and reached the FA Cup semi-final with Preston North End. In 1889, he turned professional with Rotherham Town, the home of his wife, Emma, although he had at least one child with her sister, Martha.

He played his final professional match for Stockport County in 1902, and sunk into sadness. Detached from his wife and daughter, unable to return to Africa, and troubled by ill health including alcoholism, he died in penury in Rotherham.

On 16 October 2014, a 16ft bronze statue of Arthur was unveiled at St George's Park, the training headquarters of the England football team, after a long campaign to gain him recognition led by Darlington businessman Shaun Campbell.

('Memories', *The Northern Echo*, 2007 and 2014)

30 March

At Hundens Lane, in front of a crowd of 2,000, Darlington Quaker Ladies scored their most emphatic victory over their rivals, Terry's Chocolate Girls of York, in their traditional Good Friday match, winning 10–1.

The Quaker Ladies were formed in 1925 by Lily Galloway. They practised on waste ground near Five Arches Bridge and sometimes at Feethams, playing their home games at the Railway Athletic ground in Brinkburn Road. In 1930, the Council of Christian Witness condemned the 'degrading display' of the Darlington women footballers, and so Pathé News began filming their matches. In 1932, with Galloway now manager, the Ladies – nicknamed 'the Fighting Quakers' – played what became an annual fixture against the Chocolate Girls for the first time. The York side won the first two encounters 4–2, but in 1934, the Quakers inflicted a thrashing on the visitors. Priscilla Roddham whacked in 5, Olive Pattison scored a hat-trick and Greta 'Jackie' Plews and Hannah Britton were also on the scoresheet. In the 1936 match, which the Quakers won, the crowd was a record 10,000, with proceeds going to the National Union of Railwaymen's Orphans Fund.

On 11 June 1938, Darlington stars Roddham and Plews (3) scored all the goals as England women beat Scotland 4–2 in a greyhound stadium in Newcastle. Then war came, and the footballing fun stopped.

('Memories', *The Northern Echo*, 2006 and 2007, and www.donmouth.co.uk)

20 October

Arthur Henderson – Mayor of Darlington, Nobel Peace Prize winner, first Labour member of a British Government, and partial founder of Newcastle United FC – died in London, aged 72.

A huge figure in Labour politics, 'Uncle Arthur' co-wrote Clause IV of the party's constitution, which committed it to nationalisation. He served as Foreign Secretary and Home Secretary, and was twice party leader.

Henderson was born in Glasgow but moved when he was 8 years old to Newcastle with his parents. He became an apprentice moulder with Robert Stephenson and Company, and, a keen sportsman, founded St Paul's, which was one of the football clubs that eventually united to form the Magpies. He came to Clifton Road, Darlington, in 1895 to be agent to the Liberal MP for Barnard Castle, Sir Joseph Whitwell Pease. Henderson was elected to Darlington council in 1898 as a 'progressive', and became mayor in 1903 – his term of office included the opening of the town's electric tram system.

When Sir Joseph died, Henderson was elected as Barnard Castle's Labour MP. He made history by joining Herbert Asquith's coalition government during the First World War, was a senior figure in Ramsay MacDonald's first Labour government in 1924, and devoted much of his later years to pursuing the cause which he felt would help workers most: international peace. For that, he won the Nobel Peace Prize.

('Memories', *The Northern Echo*, 1998)

6 January

The German Government announced that it had hit Darlington with an air raid – the only time during the Second World War that the town was mentioned in an official enemy communiqué. It was true – the evening before, incendiary bombs had fallen at Haughton, the John Street gasworks, Rise Carr Rolling Mills and at Stivvies (the factory of Robert Stephenson and Company). High-explosive bombs had also fallen at Whessoe, Stooperdale and Faverdale.

This was the only one of the Germans' ten raids on the town that was not preceded by air-raid sirens. Usually Darlington was targeted by lost or lone bombers, and didn't suffer any human casualties – although a number of chickens were killed when a bomb struck High Linhams in Blackwell on 1 May 1942.

On several occasions, though, Lord Haw-Haw, the notorious turncoat broadcaster, mentioned Darlington; most chillingly on 5 May 1940, when he announced that the opening of the town's new £342,000 electricity power station on Haughton Road had made it a target for German bombers. In an attempt to prove his omnipresence, Haw-Haw added that 'Darlington Town Hall Clock' was two minutes slow. Everyone rushed out and looked at the town clock, next to the town hall and, amazingly, it was.

('Memories', *The Northern Echo*, 1998, and *Listening to Britain: Home Intelligence Reports in Britain's Finest Hour*).

8 April

Starfish site 'Darlington 48A, Great Burdon' was last mentioned in operational documents. It was a SF – 'special fire' – site designed to fool German bombers into thinking that the town below them was already on fire so they should pour their bombs on top to complete the job. However, in reality, the Starfish site was a decoy burning in an empty field, located on the route bombers were most likely to take as they flew inland, having razed Middlesbrough.

Darlington 48A is first mentioned in operational documents on 1 August 1941, and it was maintained by the Royal Air Force stationed at Middleton St George. It would have taken fourteen people – one sergeant, two corporals and eleven airmen – to operate the special incendiary effects designed by Shepperton Studios. They used steel tanks, pipes, troughs and grids which made their fuel – oil, paraffin or creosote – pour, trickle or spray onto a source of ignition at timed intervals so that it blew up in different colours to convince the enemy that it was a town on fire.

The men controlled their explosions from a concrete blockhouse. No one knows how many times – if any – the site was fired.

A second Starfish site at Eryholme is now completely lost. In 2003, the mysterious concrete remains of Darlington 48A's blockhouse were designated as an Ancient Monument.

('Memories', *The Northern Echo*, 2003)

1943

6 October

Ignatius Timothy Trebitsch-Lincoln, the former Darlington MP, died in Shanghai General Hospital. He was the most preposterous conman ever elected to the House of Commons – although he remains the only British MP to become a member of the German Government.

Hungarian by birth, he wormed his way into the affections of the Liberal Rowntree family of York who backed his candidacy in Darlington in January 1910. He unseated the Conservative MP, Herbert Pike Pease, by twenty-nine votes, and set about defrauding his supporters and annoying foreign governments. When Parliament collapsed in December 1910, scandals and debts prevented him from standing again, and Darlington returned to Pike Pease.

During the First World War, Trebitsch-Lincoln tried to sell false information to both the British and German governments and then, wanted by most of Europe's police for everything from stolen gold watches to espionage, he fled to the US, where he sold his ludicrously untrue story of life as a double agent to the *New York World*.

In 1920, he became the Minister for Information in the German Kapp government, and then converted to an obscure sect of Buddhism. In China, he acquired thirteen disciples, but they deserted him when they found him in a compromising position with a young nun.

New research suggests that the Nazis might have poisoned him in Shanghai.

('Memories', *The Northern Echo*, 1990–2011)

13 June

At thirteen minutes after midnight, Lancaster KB726 VRA, from RAF Middleton St George, was caught in searchlights as it crossed the French coast, and three bullets from a Junkers fighter ripped into its port engines, setting fire to its fuselage. As it spiralled down to 1,300ft, the pilot, Art de Breyne, ordered his five-man Canadian crew to bail out. They were on their thirteenth mission together. The mid-upper gunner, Pilot Officer Andrew Mynarski, was about to jump when he noticed through the flames that rear gunner Flying Officer Pat Brophy was stuck in his glass turret. Mynarski turned, crawled through the flames and, as his flying suit ignited, made desperate attempts to break the dome and set his condemned friend free.

It was impossible. Brophy desperately gesticulated for Mynarski to save himself and, fully alight, the 27-year-old saluted and jumped. It was too late – his parachute didn't have time to open and Mynarski died on the ground of his injuries and burns.

Miraculously, as the Lancaster bomber ploughed into trees, the mechanism on Brophy's turret released, catapulting him into the air. He survived, with barely a scratch.

Two years later, Mynarski was posthumously awarded the Victoria Cross – only the second Canadian airman to receive the award, and one of the very few to win it on the uncorroborated account of a single witness.

('Memories', *The Northern Echo*, 2005)

13 January

At 5.47 p.m., Lancaster KB793 left RAF Goosepool at Middleton St George on a training exercise over the North York Moors. The Canadian crew had been together for some time, but the pilot, William McMullen, from Toronto, was flying his first proper mission.

At 2,500ft over Middlesbrough, he noticed sparks coming from the outer port engine, followed by a sheet of flame. He ordered his crew to bail out – just as they had done over France recently when they had lost their previous pilot.

The engineer, Sergeant 'Lew' Lewellin was last out. He asked Pilot Officer McMullen why he was remaining at the controls. 'It's only me for it,' he replied. 'There are thousands down below.' Darlingtonians, alerted by the unusual sound of a distressed engine, came rushing from their homes. They saw the port wing well ablaze and the plane flying in broad, downward circles until, at about 600ft, it abruptly nosedived.

McMullen stayed with it, fighting to steer it away from the houses until, at 8.49 p.m., it plunged into a Lingfield Farm field. He was killed instantly, but no one else was harmed.

'For sheer self-sacrificing heroism, your husband's action will be remembered and honoured by the people of Darlington for years to come,' wrote the mayor, Jimmy Blumer, to widow Thelma McMullen and her 5-year-old daughter, Donna Mae, in Toronto.

('Memories', *The Northern Echo*, 2005)

5 March

A stray German fighter followed the Great North Road from the south and attacked Darlington. 'It was practically hedgehopping along the road,' said a motorcyclist. 'I saw black crosses, swastikas and all. I could see that the cockpit canopy was open and the pilot gave a sort of wave – a derisive up yours wave.'

The plane flew up Northgate, firing at the old police station in Chesnut Street. It hit the St John Ambulance room on Station Road where it sliced a trombone in two, and it nearly scored a double top on the dartboard in the Builders Arms, near the Hopetown Cut, before firing at a train on the cutting bridge.

'My bedroom seemed to flash with lights and the noise was terrifying,' said Lillian Hay in 1991. 'I was 16 years old, living in Hopetown Lane. I thought the whole German air force had arrived.'

As it headed north, another of its bullets singed the cheek of a 17-year-old girl as she slept in her bed near St Paul's church. When she awoke, she discovered the bullet had passed through her pillow about two inches from her head.

In the early 1950s, a routine inspection of Darlington's iconic clock tower revealed that its weathervane had two bullet holes in it, probably from this strafing spree. The vane was replaced by one in the shape of Locomotion No. 1.

('Memories', *The Northern Echo*, 1991)

3 April

Alf Common, the first £1,000 footballer, died at his home in Coniscliffe Road. His first club was his native Sunderland, but he transferred to Sheffield United in 1901, won the FA Cup and then returned to Roker Park for a club record of £520.

But Middlesbrough were in terrible trouble near the foot of the First Division and, after two months of negotiation, paid £1,000 for the striker. The country considered it scandalous that such a huge fee should be paid for a mere footballer and questions were asked in the House of Commons. The Boro were accused of buying success.

Common's debut, on 25 February 1905, was at Sheffield United, and he scored the game's only goal – a penalty. It started a revival that enabled Middlesbrough to escape relegation.

However, Boro were a scandalously run club, accused of bribing opponents, making illegal payments and hovering on the verge of bankruptcy. In September 1907, Common, who won 3 England caps, was stripped of the captaincy and fined £10 for 'drunkenness and violent behaviour'. In August 1910, after scoring 65 goals in 178 appearances, he was given a free transfer to Arsenal providing he didn't claim the £250 Boro owed him in benefit money.

He retired to Darlington in 1919 and became well known as a pub landlord, first at the Cleaver in Skinnergate and then the Alma in Cockerton.

('Memories', *The Northern Echo*, 1992)

17 December

Private Brian Chandler, 20, was the last person to be executed at Durham, after he killed an 83-year-old woman in Darlington – for £4.

Chandler had hooked up with two teenage girls after going AWOL from Catterick. They stole a bike and shoplifted, and then one of the girls mentioned that she had done some cleaning for Martha Dodd who always kept £200 in her home at No. 4, Victoria Road.

On 11 June, Chandler subjected Mrs Dodd to 'a savage and prolonged attack', killing her with nineteen hammer blows to the head. In court, he at first claimed that he had acted in self-defence; then he claimed that one of the girls – 'a strapping young woman' who could have appeared in *I Was A Teenage Werewolf*, said his barrister – had done it.

On 27 October, the jury took little more than an hour to find him guilty, and he died twenty-one days later. 'The execution attracted little public interest in Durham,' reported *The Northern Echo*. 'The walls surrounding the gardens outside the prison were bare of the normal gathering of onlookers, and as the hands of the clock on the prison tower reached 9am, the hour fixed for the execution, the scene outside remained deserted except for a group of reporters standing in the rain.'

The death penalty was abolished in December 1964.

('Memories', *The Northern Echo*, 1995)

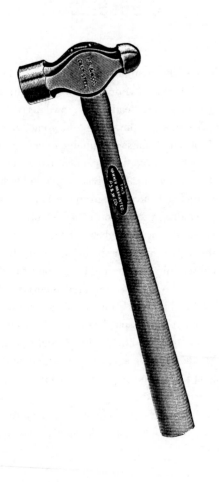

8 December

'A full house of 1,100 screaming teenagers attended Darlington's Civic Theatre's first beat concert last night,' said *The Northern Echo*. 'Outside there were Beatle-type crowds as police, time and time again, cleared a way through for the great guitar heroes.'

Hundreds of female fans were unable to get into the Five By Five show, which featured five local beat bands, each with five members. This was the peak of 'Beatmania' in Darlington. Top of the bill were The Concordes, from the Majestic in Bondgate where they usually backed groups like Manfred Mann, Unit Four Plus Two and The Merseybeats. They, and their co-stars at the Civic, the Vipers, had recently played with The Searchers – top of the charts with 'Needles and Pins' – on a Shildon pitheap.

Jet Storme and the Cyclones appeared as advertised at the Five By Five show, but The Foot-Tappers fell out with the organisers and The Three Pin Square split days before the big gig. Therefore, the line-up was completed by the Black Nights, from the Lyric cinema in Middleton St George, and Derek Saint and the Sinners. 'Fans go wild at big beat bonanza', reported the *Echo*. 'Wonderful, wonderful fare for the kids.'

When The Concordes split in September 1965 to go to college, more than 700 young fans in a week signed a petition demanding they re-form.

('Memories', *The Northern Echo*, 2005)

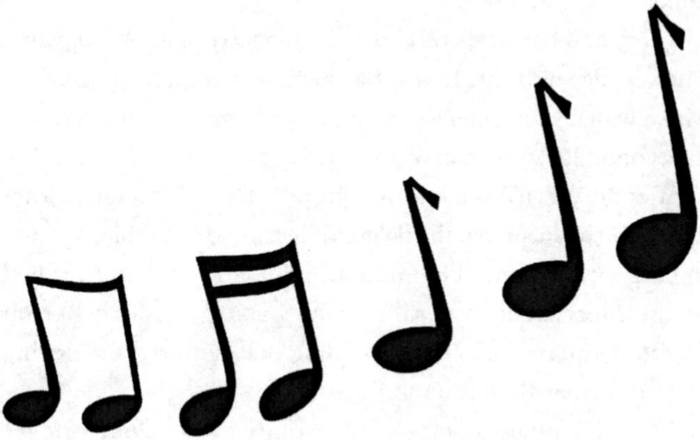

15 May

Tom Fraser, the Minister of Transport, opened the 10½-mile Darlington bypass motorway – the A1(M) – and the 2-mile Spur Link road – the A66(M).

There had been talk of bypassing the town since 1929, when a new bridge over the Tees at Blackwell was proposed to connect with a widened Carmel Road, but this scheme was scuppered by the economic depression of the 1930s.

After the war, a motorway was proposed from Kneeton Corner, near Scotch Corner, to the delightfully named Crumbley Corner in County Durham. The route would follow the old trackbed of the Merrybent mineral railway, passing through Barton limestone quarry. The only building that required bulldozing was the former Barton station.

The 12½ miles of motorway required thirty-four bridges, 3.75 million cubic yards of earthworks and the alteration of 9½ miles of side roads. The controversial Conservative Minister of Transport, Ernest Marples, cut the first sod in May 1963, but following the 1964 General Election, it was his Labour successor who declared the £6.5 million project open. For the first time since the Romans had bypassed Darlington nearly 2,000 years earlier, the town was no longer on the main highway between London and Edinburgh.

However, in Stapleton, where the A66(M) had removed all the traffic, residents complained that they could no longer get to sleep because their village was too quiet.

(F.A. Sims: *The Motorway Achievement: Building
the Network in the North-East of England*)

2 April

North Road Shops, which at their peak in 1954 employed 4,000 men, shut on this day despite noisy protests and processions on High Row.

The shops were a victim of the Beeching Axe, a brutal efficiency programme that cut 6,000 miles of railway – a third of the country's mileage – with a devastating knock-on effect on the men who built and maintained the rolling stock.

William Bouch, the Stockton and Darlington Railway's resident engineer, had opened North Road on 1 January 1863. It contained a repair shop, erecting shop, heavy machine shop, wheel shop, hydraulic shop, boiler shop, flanging and tube repairing shop, brass finishing shop, wheel-turning shop and a plate bending and straightening shop as well as shops for joiners, patternmakers, millwrights, tinsmiths, coppersmiths and brassmoulders.

'It may be noted,' noted a 1903 workshop booklet, 'that all the artificial limbs – the use of which among railway employees misfortune too often rends necessary – are made in this shop.'

Between 1863 and 1957, North Road made 2,269 steam engines; from 1952 to 1964, it built 187 diesel shunters. With its closure, Darlington (population: 85,000) had lost at least 7,000 railway jobs in ten years as the Stooperdale boilershop, the Faverdale wagon works and 'Stivvies' – Robert Stephenson and Company – had also gone as the age of the train came to an end.

('Memories', *The Northern Echo*, 2006)

2 February

Jimi Hendrix played at the Blue Pad Club in the Imperial Hotel – the most famous night in Darlington's rock history. The gig ended with an enduring mystery: what happened to his Fender Stratocaster guitar?

Hendrix was booked for a fee of £90 when he was an unknown, but as the gig drew near, his first single, 'Hey Joe', burst into the Top Ten. His record company offered £300 to cancel the show, but his manager, Geordie Chaz Chandler from The Animals, insisted it should go ahead.

The *Evening Despatch*'s Allene James commented:

> About 200 young people stopped dancing and crowded around the platform to see the man himself at work. One couldn't deny that this artiste is a colourful one, both in his dress and comments, and in an interview after his performance he told me: 'The group and I have only been together since September and, yeah man, we're pretty happy about our present position in the charts.'

Perhaps while she was speaking to him, Hendrix's black guitar was stolen. It was said to have been whisked down the Imperial fire escape, and sprayed cream overnight. Some sources say that when Hendrix discovered the theft, he stormed into the downstairs Bolivar bar in a rage; others that he was phlegmatic and said: 'I hope the dude can play.'

('Memories', *The Northern Echo*, 2005)

27 May

Princess Anne officially opened Darlington's new town hall and unveiled the sculpture outside. The town hall, designed by Newcastle architects Williamson, Faulkner Brown and Partners along with borough architect Eric Tornbohm, was supposed to be the first phase in a questionable concept to cover the town centre with glass and concrete civic boxes. Fortunately, it never happened.

The sculpture, by Cheltenham artist John Hoskin, is called 'Resurgence' and symbolises Darlington's escape from industrial decline. It was not universally popular, with letters to *The Northern Echo* describing it as 'an ambitious abortion in steel' (it is actually made of zinc with stainless steel blades) and saying that a new public toilet would have been preferable.

Despite thigh-high boots and a short miniskirt, the demure princess looked as if butter wouldn't melt in her mouth as she unveiled the sculpture. But Monty Python comedian Michael Palin, in his *Halfway to Hollywood* diaries, wrote a strange entry dated 2 November 1980:

> I have a glass of wine, sign some autographs and meet Kate Adie – a rather dynamic lady who tells me that she was with Princess Anne unveiling something in Darlington. It turned out to be a particularly unprepossessing plaque to 'The Spirit of New Darlington' and, as everyone applauded, Princess Anne leaned over to Kate Adie and muttered a heartfelt: 'F*** me!'

('Memories', *The Northern Echo*, 2012)

25 September

A three-day Northern Ireland peace conference began at the newly opened Europa Lodge Hotel (now Blackwell Grange).

Northern Ireland Secretary William Whitelaw led the talks between a dozen moderate Ulster politicians – the Nationalists and Revd Ian Paisley boycotted the event. Whitelaw was assisted by a large secretariat and 150 police officers, and scrutinised by 200 journalists.

Although it wasn't regarded as significant at the time, the Darlington conference agreed that while Northern Ireland should remain part of the UK for as long as the people wanted it to, a way forward would be to give 'minority interests a share in the exercise of executive power' – the start of 'power-sharing'. 'There was only one snag,' Whitelaw said later in his memoirs. 'The hotel was surrounded by a golf course which would have to be closed for the conference.'

This disappointed Whitelaw, a keen golfer, as the only 'golfers' on the course were undercover security men taking part in the biggest such operation ever undertaken in Britain – 1972 was one of the deadliest years of the Troubles, with more than 450 people killed.

However, 'the Blackwell Grange Golf Club ... was generous enough to make me an honorary member', and Whitelaw returned for a round when he was guest at the local Conservative Association ball in September 1974.

('Memories', *The Northern Echo*, 1999)

25 November

Four arsonists, aged between 10 and 14, broke into St Paul's church on North Road and, using candles and leaves, set fire to the 101-year-old building. It took twenty firemen two hours to bring the blaze under control, but it was too late – the church had to be demolished, so cutting Darlington's connection to the greatest royal scandal of the twentieth century.

On 30 May 1937, the Revd Robert Anderson Jardine, the vicar of St Paul's, disappeared from the church. He reappeared on 3 June at the Chateau de Cande, near Tours in France, where he married the Duke of Windsor – who had recently abdicated as King Edward VIII – to Mrs Wallis Simpson, the twice-divorced American socialite who had cost the king his crown.

After the service, the vicar motored back to St Paul's where, on 5 June, he married George and Doris Gamble. More than 700 people crammed into the church, with US camera crews outside among the crowds. The vicar explained that he believed no one should be denied a Christian wedding, and he gave the happy couple a slice of the royal wedding cake. He told them: 'I shall now put this book away and it will not be used any more after today. You have had exactly the same service, word for word, as the Duke and Duchess at the chateau.'

('Memories', *The Northern Echo*, 1993–2011)

23 June

In the 33rd minute of a World Cup match against Poland, Darlington-born Giuseppe Wilson won his third, and final, cap for Italy.

Giuseppe, the captain of Lazio whom he had helped to their first Serie A league title, came on as a substitute to play alongside such legendary Azzurri names as Dino Zoff and Fabio Capello. Yet he'd been born Joseph Wilson on 27 October 1945, in Arnold Road. His father, Dennis, who worked at Darlington Forge, had been on wartime service in Italy where he had met Lina d'Francesca. They had returned to Darlington and married, but Lina couldn't settle in the Darlington winters, so with the baby six months old, they started anew in Italy.

Joseph interrupted his law studies at university to do fifteen months' national service so he could claim Italian citizenship, and he changed his name to Giuseppe. He joined Internapoli and then Lazio in 1969, for whom he made a record 324 appearances at left back, missing only 6 games in 11 years, and scoring 6 goals.

Nicknamed 'Pino', he made his international debut in a friendly before the 1974 World Cup in which he made two substitute appearances, the last of which was against Poland. However, Italy lost 2–1 and were eliminated amid great Italian angst. Giuseppe's international career was over.

(*The Northern Echo* 1992 and FIFA database)

19 October

Station B, Darlington's electricity power station that dominated the townscape with three huge, squat cooling towers and three tall, slender chimneys, stopped generating.

At least one man was killed during the construction of the brick cooling towers, which replaced Station A, in early 1940. When B began generating in May 1940, Lord Haw-Haw announced that Darlington was now a target for German bombers. Perhaps as a response, some people remember the cooling towers, off Haughton Road, being painted with camouflage.

The station was nationalised in 1948, and in 1950 the British Electricity Authority promised the people of the Bank Top area of town that it would do something about the station's 'artificial drizzle'. Steam from the towers mixed with vapours from the slender chimneys, which then mingled with smoke from the trains on the mainline to produce a continuous fine shower, rendering it impossible for housewives to hang white clothes in their backyards.

The problem was not resolved until 1976 when the station was shut, having only contributed to the National Grid at peak times for three years. The demolition of the towers on 28 January 1979, solved another problem: people all over town reported that their colour television reception improved enormously. The three chimneys were demolished one by one in 1982.

('Memories', *The Northern Echo*, 2009)

24 March

Labour's Ossie O'Brien won a by-election and became Darlington MP for just eleven weeks and one day – the fifth shortest term of office in Parliamentary history.

O'Brien's father had been disabled during the First World War and his mother was a Peases' mill girl. When 14, he reputedly lied about his age to join the Royal Navy. He later attended college in Birmingham and then Durham University.

His first bid to be selected as Labour's Darlington candidate in 1965 failed by one vote. The winner, Edward 'Ted' Fletcher, went on to hold the seat until his death in 1983. In the subsequent by-election, O'Brien beat Michael Fallon, a 30-year-old Scottish Conservative, by 2,412 votes. But just seventy-seven days later, with Margaret Thatcher riding high after the Falklands victory, O'Brien fought the General Election on a Labour manifesto described as 'the longest suicide note in history'. He lost to Fallon by 3,438 votes.

When O'Brien's wait to be sworn in and the four-week election campaign are discounted, his parliamentary career lasted just forty-five days.

After his death in 1997, renowned left-wing Labour MP Tam Dalyell wrote: 'But for the verdict of the electorate and the ill luck 18 years earlier of such a close selection conference result, he would undoubtedly have made a serious contribution to Parliament in the field of education and training.'

(*The Independent*, 1997)

1989

2 June

This was the last day of the public inquiry into Stage V – the final stage – of Darlington's £4.2 million inner ring road. Stage V was to start at Bondgate, smash through Salt Yard, cut Duke Street in half, whizz through Larchfield Street with huge sound baffles protecting the ears of Stanhope Road residents, and then bash its way through Coniscliffe Road to a mega-roundabout where Grange Road joins Victoria Road. It would have completed the circle started in the late 1960s, although the concept had blighted properties in the area since 1948.

'This is the last chance for the townscape of Darlington,' English Heritage's barrister William Hicks told the government inspectors. 'We urge you to cut off that noose and throw it away and allow enhancement to start.'

The inspectors delivered their historic rejection on 2 July 1990. It was the first time a road had been rejected on purely historic and environmental grounds, and is seen as a landmark case. The judgement further strained relations between Durham County Council, which had spent £625,000 buying land for the road, and Darlington Borough Council, which was at best lukewarm towards the project and was desperate for independence from Durham (it became a unitary authority in 1994). It also explains why Darlington has a ring road that doesn't form a ring – or a noose.

(*The Northern Echo*, 1989–1990)

30 June

'The Cocker Beck flowing through the heart of Darlington yesterday turned bright green, then black and later bright blue before finishing the day light brown,' reported *The Northern Echo*.

It wasn't the first time that the beck had hit the headlines for the wrong reasons – 'Beck burps obnoxious green slime', said the *Echo* on 17 February 1989 – and it wasn't the last. Even though the source of the coloured contaminants was quickly traced to a printing factory, things soon got much nastier. On 7 August, the park gates were bolted in the interests of public health after floating foreign bodies were found. 'The beck is running raw sewage,' a resident was quoted as saying.

Investigations discovered that blocked sewers as far away as Elton Road and Milbank Road were causing sewage to run into rainwater channels that flowed into the beck. The pollution was compounded by scores of washing machines in the nearby terraces which had been wrongly plumbed in – some of them for as long as fifty years.

After an eight-month clean-up, mayor Barrie Lamb ceremonially reopened the Denes on 6 April 1990, and the beck was so clean that four months later police warned takeaway shops to be certain of their salad sources after groups of Oriental-looking women were reportedly seen collecting bagfuls of wild watercress from its banks.

(Lloyd: *The History of the Denes of Darlington*)

2 September

Weighing 6lb 11oz and born at 5.55 a.m., baby Chelsea Pattinson – daughter of Carol and David, who supported a London football team – was the last of about 50,000 Darlingtonians to be born at Greenbank Maternity Hospital.

The hospital opened on the site of a mansion called Greenbank on 6 February 1885. It was designed by G.G. Hoskins, and its £11,000 cost was covered by townspeople who held an annual Hospital Sunday in their churches, and a week-long bazaar. Greenbank remained the town's main hospital until 1933, when Darlington Memorial opened. From then on it concentrated on maternity services, acquiring a £30,000 antenatal clinic in 1971. In 1989, a £1.75 million maternity unit opened at the Memorial on the day Greenbank closed, and so the first Memorial baby shared a birthday with Chelsea. He was Gregory Milward, born at 9.50 p.m., weighing 6lb 6oz.

Just as babies transferred to the new site, so did the statue of the Pharoah's daughter discovering baby Moses in the bulrushes. Beautifully carved by Giovanni Battista Lombardi in Rome in the 1870s, it had stood majestically in Rockliffe Hall, the home of Alfred and Rachel Backhouse in Hurworth until March 1899, when it was presented to Greenbank in memory of the banking couple who had given much money to Darlington hospitals. It still stands at the maternity ward entrance.

(*The Northern Echo*, 1989, and Lloyd: *Rockliffe*)

3 November

'Dizzy', performed by the Wonderstuff and comedian Vic Reeves, who was known as James Roderick Moir when he grew up in Darlington, went to No 1.

Reeves' family moved to Hewitson Road from Leeds in 1964 when he was 5. His father, James, was a linotype operator at *The Northern Echo*, and Vic remembered seeing his fast fingers 'spreading across the keys like lightning'. Vic attended Eastbourne primary and secondary schools, and let his imagination run wild digging 'space pits' on Yarm Road wasteland, from which he would make-believe he was an alien.

He shopped in Darlington's alternative stores. 'Guru was great,' he told *The Northern Echo* in 2006. 'I once bought a pair of white flares, split at the knee, but I dyed them green very quickly. They were only £1.99.' He bought his first guitar, a Gibson EB3, from William's music shop, and formed a band called Trout, or The Fashionable Five, which played at the Green Dragon in Post House Wynd and the Bowes cellar bar on Skinnergate.

After school, Reeves worked at Neasham market garden, where one of his duties was castrating piglets. But the bright lights of London beckoned. He teamed up with Middlesbrough solicitor Bob Mortimer and their *Big Night Out* comedy programme became a cult hit in the early 1990s.

(Reeves: *Me: Moir*, Virgin Books, 2006)

27 August

The £60 million Cornmill shopping centre was opened by the Mayor of Darlington, Councillor David Lyonette. It radically reshaped the heart of the town, sweeping away a hodgepodge of shops and back yards. The biggest loss was the Co-op store, which stretched from Priestgate to Tubwell Row. It had closed in April 1986, making 112 people redundant and leaving Priestgate without a co-operative for the first time since the formation of the Priestgate Co-operative and Industrial Society in 1868.

Foundations for the Cornmill had to be sunk 60ft because of the shifting riverside soil. In May 1989, a leg of a 90-ton crane snapped, leaving the vehicle in danger of collapse, and so the town centre had to be evacuated. In February 1990, a workman, 55-year-old Ralph Collins of Guisborough, died after falling from scaffolding.

Some likened the appearance of the shopping centre to 'a Second World War concentration camp'. Chief architect Stephen Gray said: 'Cornmill is designed to reflect various aspects of existing buildings in Darlington, although not to copy them slavishly.' He was particularly proud of his glass atrium, which is the centrepiece of the centre.

The mall was called 'Cornmill' because in ancient times the Bishop of Durham sited the town corn mill where the TK Maxx multi-storey car park is today.

(*The Northern Echo*, 1992)

11 November

Darlington Transport Company (DTC) withdrew its last thirty buses and made its fifty staff redundant after going into liquidation with debts of £300,000. It had lost the 'Darlington bus wars', which began in 1986 when Margaret Thatcher's government deregulated the bus industry. This caused Darlington council to turn DTC, formed in 1925, into a standalone company. It had sixty-two buses and 145 employees, and was valued at more than £3 million.

In September 1994, Stagecoach, part of a national chain that had 6,300 buses and 13,000 employees, became interested, which forced the council to put DTC out to competitive tender. Of eleven interested parties, Yorkshire Traction of Barnsley bid the highest: £1.5 million, appreciably more than Stagecoach's £1,033,333. In retaliation, Stagecoach poached DTC's drivers – sixty of DTC's eighty-eight drivers were lured by the offer of £1,000 bonuses and three-year contracts – and Yorkshire Traction withdrew.

On 7 November, Stagecoach flooded the town with free buses. More than 300 buses an hour, of all shapes, sizes and colours, entered the town centre; the streets were littered with temporary bus stops; the roads were full of bus-drivers leapfrogging each other, and opposition football fans at Feethams sang: 'Darlo, Darlo, give us a bus!'

This drove DTC into liquidation. In March 1995, the Competition Commission branded Stagecoach's actions 'predatory, deplorable and against the public interest'.

(*The Northern Echo*, 1994–96)

31 March

Dressers of High Row shut, ending nearly 200 years of retailing history. The firm was started in 1809 when John Readman, of Stockton, set up as a printer in Priestgate. After 1825, he became the house printer for the new Stockton and Darlington Railway so when he retired in 1849, the Peases selected a young Quaker from Brighton, Harrison Penney, as his replacement. Penney immediately appointed an apprentice: William Dresser, 16, from Bondgate.

Once qualified, William went into business on his own in High Row, investing in an early atmospheric gas engine to power his press. 'It was a fearsome contraption of ratchets, cog-wheels, explosions and smells, and people came from near and far to see it,' said a witness.

William's first apprentice was Joseph Malaby Dent, from Archer Street, who qualified in 1867 and went to London to set up the famous Everyman's books. In 1888, William bought out Penney, and traded at the north end of High Row. His sons sold out in 1953, but Dressers kept its family feel while expanding its lines. In 1966, it moved into its landmark premises, which had just been vacated by Richard Luck and Sons, a haberdashery founded in 1783. With glass-fronted display cases and a grand sweeping staircase, Dressers of High Row was redolent of old-fashioned retailing – you could buy anything and everything there.

('Memories', *The Northern Echo*, 2001)

15 August

The biggest fire for years in Darlington broke out at 12.40 a.m. on the top floor of the King's Head Hotel in Prebend Row. Sixty firefighters, ten fire engines and a police helicopter took six hours to get it under control, although the 100-plus guests – from China, India, Italy and Canada – were ushered out unharmed. A quarter of the building was destroyed and it stood covered by a large tarpaulin for several years while investigations were carried out. Arson was suspected, but no culprit was ever traced.

The hotel fully reopened in 2012, so splendidly restored that a casual observer would never know how badly G.G. Hoskins' Gothic masterpiece had been ravaged.

The King's Head was first mentioned in 1661. It became the town's premier coaching inn – in 1762, landlady Isabella Stephenson advertised that she had 'good post chaises, able horses and careful drivers', and she assured 'noblemen, gentlemen and others of meeting with the civilest entertainments'. The railways ended the coaching era, and the last Newcastle to London stagecoach left the King's Head in October 1852.

In 1890, Sunderland brewers R. Fenwick and Company bought the seventeenth-century hotel for £7,000 and demolished it, allowing architect Hoskins to create what *The Northern Echo* described on opening day – 1 June 1893 – as 'a palatial hotel' and a 'temple of luxury'.

('Memories', *The Northern Echo*, 2003, 2008–2012)

Bibliography

Books

Addison, Paul, and Crang, Jeremy A., *Listening to Britain: Home Intelligence Reports in Britain's Finest Hour* (Vintage, 2011)

Cookson, Gillian (ed.), *The Victoria History of the County of Durham Volume IV: Darlington* (Boydell & Brewster, 2005)

Flynn, George, *The Book of Darlington* (Barracuda Books, 1987)

Kirby, M.W., *Men of Business and Politics* (George Allen & Unwin, 1984)

Lloyd, Chris, *A History of the Denes of Darlington* (Friends of the Denes, 2012)

——, *A Walk in the Park* (*The Northern Echo*, 2005)

——, *Attacking the Devil: 130 Years of The Northern Echo* (*The Northern Echo*, 2000)

——, *Memories of Darlington Volumes 1-3* (*The Northern Echo*, 1992–2001)

——, *Of Fish and Actors: 100 Years of Darlington Civic Theatre* (*The Northern Echo*, 2007)

——, *The Road to Rockliffe* (*The Northern Echo*, 2010)

Lockwood, Stephen, *Darlington Trolleybuses including the Tramways* (Middleton Press, 2004)

Longstaffe ,William, *The History and Antiquities of Darlington* (*Darlington and Stockton Times*, 1854)

Malmesbury, James Howard Harris, *Memoirs of an Ex-Minister* (1884)

Moore, Wendy, *Wedlock: How Georgian Britain's Worst Husband Met His Match* (Orion, 2009)

Nicholson, C.P., *Those Boys o' Bondgate* (Darlington and Teesdale Field Naturalists Club, 1949)

Pease, Sir Alfred (ed.), *The Diaries of Edward Pease: The Father of English Railways* (Headley Brothers, 1907)

Reeves, Vic, *Me: Moir* (Virgin Books, 2006)

Robinson, W. Sydney, *Muckraker: the Scandalous Life and Times of W.T. Stead* (Robson Press, 2012)

Sims, F.A., *The Motorway Achievement: Building the Network in the North-East of England* (Phillimore & Co., 2009)

Van Tilburg, Jo Anne, *Among Stone Giants: The Life of Katherine Routledge and Her Remarkable Expedition to Easter Island* (Scribner, 2003)

Wall, John, *First in the World: The Stockton and Darlington Railway* (Sutton Publishing, 2001)

Wasserstein, Bernard, The Secret Lives of Trebitsch-Lincoln (Yale University Press, 1988)

Newspapers

Darlington and Stockton Times
Northern/Evening Despatch
North Star
The Independent
The Northern Echo

Websites

www.donmouth.co.uk

Also from The History Press

GREAT WAR BRITAIN

Great War Britain is a unique new local series to mark the centenary of the Great War. In partnership with archives and museums across Great Britain, the series provides an evocative portrayal of life during this 'war to end all wars'. In a scrapbook style, and beautifully illustrated, it includes features such as personal memoirs, letters home, diary extracts, newspaper reports, photographs, postcards and other local First World War ephemera.

Find these titles and more at
www.thehistorypress.co.uk

Also from The History Press

HAUNTED

This series is sure to petrify everyone interested in the ghostly history of their hometown. Containing a terrifying collection of spine-chilling tales, from spooky sightings in pubs and theatres to paranormal investigations in cinemas and private homes, each book in the series is guaranteed to appeal to both serious ghost hunters and those who simply fancy a fright.

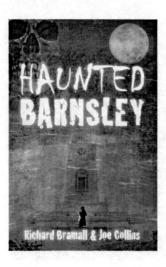

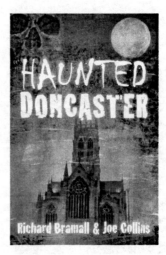

Also from The History Press

MURDER & CRIME

This series brings together numerous murderous tales from history. Featuring cases of infanticide, drowning, shooting and stabbing, amongst many other chilling killings, these well-illustrated and enthralling books will appeal to everyone interested in true crime and the shadier side of their hometown's past.

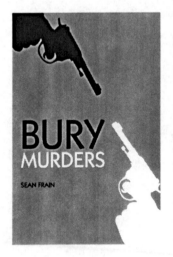

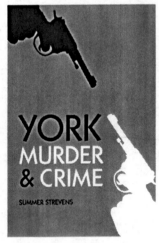

Lightning Source UK Ltd.
Milton Keynes UK
UKOW02f0146211114

241957UK00009B/76/P